Tim Kelly

Master of
Stage Fright

The Life & Times of America's
Most Prolific Playwright

BY BEN OHMART

Published in the USA by:
BearManor Media
P O Box 71426
Albany, Georgia 31708
www.bearmanormedia.com

ISBN 1-59393-317-7

Printed in the United States of America.
Book design by Brian Pearce.

Table of Contents

Introduction

So, you might be asking: Why a book on Tim Kelly?

I'm sure there's a deep-seated psychological reason for this, but I've always admired prolific people. I started buying Frank Zappa CDs, not because I knew the music terribly well, but because there was so *much* of it. In my case, I wanted to write plays — lots of them — and I set out to conquer the theatrical world by immersing myself in the subject. I managed to have a few of my efforts produced (in Minneapolis, Australia, etc.), but I eventually began specializing in publishing books on vintage entertainment through my company, BearManor Media. Still, I love the craft of writing plays, and I think back fondly on the hours I spent poring over the Pioneer Drama catalog (with its distinctive blue cover). One byline was repeated again and again throughout the catalog's pages: "A New Play by Tim Kelly."

I ordered some of these plays and studied them. This Kelly man, I soon discovered, really knew how to construct and develop drama. His flair for detail was spot on. No, they weren't "great" plays, but they were *fun*—and I'd rather see a fun play than a great one any day. Tim's plays kept moving, they were true to *themselves*, and they were clean and family friendly. I respect that. Critics, however, did not. They dismissed the vehicles that Tim wrote for the school market. He had "sold out," they said disdainfully. ("Sold out" apparently is code for "Why are you making more money than I am?") Professional insults were lobbed his way, with such phrases as "watered-down comedy" and "second-rate dramatic writing for audiences that don't know any better."

These were cheap shots. Selling a play, after all, is no easy task. Selling a novel is easy — just publish it yourself. Ditto for short stories; plus there are a plethora of small magazines and presses out there eager for your experimentation. But a play requires a *large* collaborative body to live, even assuming you can get your toe in past that hard-to-please committee of adults (if you're shooting for the school market) who need to know that your drama or comedy will entertain as well as instruct — and do so without offending anyone, onstage or off. Try doing all that and see how many acceptance letters *you* get.

To show my appreciation for his work, I sent Tim Kelly a fan letter in 1997. In it I enclosed a series of questions, which he was kind enough to answer. (That interview is reprinted in Chapter 12 of this book.) Since Tim's untimely death in 1998 I have stayed in touch with his life partner, Roland H. Bibolet. Roland's love for Tim is evident. He was a constant support to him during their forty-one years together, and he has worked tirelessly to perpetuate his legacy. When I suggested a book on Tim's life and career, Roland provided me with hours of candid interviews and supplied dozens of previously unpublished pictures. Perhaps most significantly, he granted me permission to reprint a wide sampling of Tim's writing: articles, play synopses, theatrical reviews — even an original screenplay for the legendary Mae West.

Thank you, Roland. Without you, sir, there would be no book.

I am also grateful to the many dedicated Kelly fans for their generous assistance: Steve Fendrich, Florine Atwood, Wendell Cocking, Michael Sutton, Tom Owen, Max Wesley Harding, Celia Concannon, Jim Phillips, Jess Stacey, Lon Davis, among many others. Tim's friends and family members contributed their memories, to my everlasting gratitude. Rather than cut up their comments, I've included them in their entirety. These were the people who knew Tim best, and they say it all better than I can.

Tim Kelly succeeded mightily at what he did and that is the reason for this book. It's time he was given his due, beyond the royalties his estate continues to receive. I hope from this biography, you'll get to know Tim, the man and the writer.

He was amazing.

Ben Ohmart

"One should not approach a play as one does the movies, radio or television. One should go to the theatre as one goes to church, bringing something very personal to it."

Tim Kelly

Chapter
One

Francis Seymour Kelley (July 11, 1898–June 8, 1964) and Mary Edna Furey (July 25, 1901–March 21, 1973) were both of Irish ancestry via Prince Edward Island in Canada. They married on January 31, 1927. Tim Kelly was born October 2, 1931 in Saugus, Massachusetts. He had two sisters: Jackie Hayes, and Patricia "Patsy" K. Schultz.

> Patsy:
>
> Please bear in mind the difference in our ages — twelve and a half years. Let's start with the year I was born, 1944. When I was brought home from the hospital it was Tim who rode in the back seat of the car holding me in his arms — his five-day-old sister, while Mother was up front with Dad for the ride from Boston to Lynn. I think from that day on Tim always kept an eye out for me.
>
> The year I entered school, Tim had graduated the summer before and had enlisted in the Army. My sister was already married with her first child. I do have a few memories before 1949 though…Tim would take me to visit his friends, putting me on his bicycle. I was in front of him, seated on the crossbar of his bike.
>
> In high school Tim was active in drama. The senior class was putting on some kind of a drama, and he brought home one of the props, the head of a cow. He liked to "try things out" on me to see the reaction, and when I saw this "monster" coming at me (I didn't know he was under the prop) I screamed bloody murder, and pretty loud for a four-year-old. Other things that come to mind: hand puppets. He gave me two, one was a white rabbit

Mary and Frank Kelley, Tim's parents.

and we called him Fletcher. The other puppet was a witch with a broom in her hand. She was called Hazel. This sixteen-year-old young man always had time for [his] little four-year-old, and if he was busy with other things it was always "we'll make up for it later." Did you ever make shadow pictures with your hands and use the wall as a background, the light shining on the wall? We did a lot of that, particularly "the swan."

When Tim was a kid the family lived over a drugstore. Tim used to like to get on the phone and ask whoever answered, "Do you keep Prince Albert [Pipe tobacco] in a can?" The pharmacist would say "Yes" and Tim would answer, "Why don't you let the poor guy out to breathe?" Then hang up. He had a wacky imagination.

Tim started writing when he was about twelve years old. He entered a story in a contest using Nana's name (that's my maternal grandmother) and didn't tell anyone about it. One of Nana's friends called her to tell her that her story was published in either a newspaper or magazine; when Tim came home from school that afternoon they questioned him about it, and he said, "Yes, I wrote it and did one in mother's name, too." That one got published, too, and from that time on Tim was always writing. I'm not sure, but since Tim was using women's names here perhaps it was either a woman's magazine or column of a newspaper. I do know that as a teenager he had two stories published in the Catholic magazine called *The Liguorian*. Not sure if he used his own name there.

Summertime meant going to New Hampshire. Nana had a place up there and Tim found the summer theater in Raymond, New Hampshire. Soon he was acting and doing backstage work. Nana spent her summers in New Hampshire, but lived with us other times of the year. Our household consisted of Mother and Dad, Mother's mother, my sister Jacqueline who is the oldest, then Tim, then myself. There is a four-year difference between Jackie and Tim.

Where and when Tim started dropping the last "e" in the name Kelley I do not know — I would imagine after he started writing full time.

Around 1951 Tim was in the Army. Besides being in Georgia and Arlington, Virginia, he was also in Carlisle, Pennsylvania. I think he went to school there before being stationed in Georgia and Virginia. While stationed in Georgia he came down with malaria and recovered from that. While in Arlington the family got a call saying that he was in the Walter Reed Hospital with a sickness known as Guillen-Barre. It took him two years to recover — first he was in an iron lung, then he went into a wheelchair, then [he was using] two canes, relapsed going back to the iron lung, back to the wheelchair, two canes, one cane, then he was medically discharged and came home.

The GI Bill made it possible for Tim to go to college. He enrolled at Emerson College in Boston; took the bus and subway everyday from Lynn to Boston. He didn't drive, his legs were still

Hollywood, circa 1968. Tim, Roland, Tim's mother, Edna Kelley.

weak from the Guillen-Barre and he was a great user of public transportation.

Many times when the weather was bad in the winter and we were snowed in, Tim used me as a model for trying out his makeup. One time he made me up as a skunk. He used to practice on Mother too, (she looked elegant) and I can remember trying to always "sit still in the chair" for him. Board games (Monopoly in particular) and cards were a popular past-time, too. Many times we (Mom, Dad and I) went to see Tim in a drama while he was at Emerson, usually on a Friday night. For me that was a treat — going into town and staying up late. When Tim graduated from Emerson and got his B. A., he was Valedictorian of his class. He also got his M. A., and did this all in about five years, going to school during the summer. He was also a "student teacher."

I finished elementary school (sixth grade) and instead of going into junior high, Tim persuaded Mom and Dad to enroll me in St. Mary's for the seventh and eighth grades. He thought I would get a better education there compared to the public junior high school. One day on the way to Lynn Beach (he loved to swim in the ocean), he stopped there and spoke with the nuns about

Roland, Tim's mom, Mrs. Edna Kelly, and Tim at Pinnacle Peak, Phoenix. Undated.

enrolling me, explaining that I wore a hearing aid, always sat up front in my classes and we were members of the parish. The nuns accepted me and off I went in the fall.

Also during this same summertime Tim was concerned about my reading comic books too much, and took them away from me. "I want you to get involved in reading books [he said]. Here, take this book, read a chapter everyday and tell me what it says."

The book was *The Wizard of Oz*, and to this day I still enjoy reading.

He started teaching in New York State that fall and I was getting used to the parochial school; it was a challenge and I was having problems with English since emphasis was placed on diagramming sentences and where to place your nouns, pronouns, etc. Reports were coming home from the school and being shared with Tim via mail and phone. I do remember him telling Mother, "Ma, don't worry about this. Pat speaks wonderful English. The diagramming of sentences is not going to matter that much later on in life; she will survive." Somehow I did. (I can tell you if something sounds right, but can't tell you why).

One incident I do remember, while Tim was still a student at Emerson College. He wanted to go on the road with his drama. Dad wanted him to stay in college and finish his studies, but Tim really wanted to tour. He wrote the drama, and I think the name of it was *Road Show*. Dad put his foot down, said he didn't want Tim to become a "starving actor." [Dad] preferred that [Tim] have his degree, a firm foundation with which to support himself. After college he could do what he wanted, but at least he would have something to fall back on.

The turning point for Tim the writer came at age 12 when he received $50 for a story about a dog that went to war. "Notice: Dogs for War" was published in *Victorian* magazine and gave Tim the heady knowledge that there were people in this world that would pay him for doing what he loved. In the 1940s, fifty dollars went a long way.

"It was a wonderful thing for a kid to realize that power; I wouldn't have to work in a car wash or anything like that," Tim recalled.

Though he loved the gothic atmosphere of the works of Arthur Miller and Tennessee Williams, he was much more influenced by films, usually those with fly-sized budgets. *The Seventh Victim, I Walked with a Zombie* and *The Body Snatcher* gave him an early love for a genre that would ultimately become his trademark as a playwright.

He also took refuge in radio drama in the early fifties, (before it was killed by television), particularly *I Love a Mystery*. An avid reader, he devoured the adventure novels of Edgar Rice Burroughs, with his imaginative "other world" series. *Oz* author L. Frank Baum also occupied his time. Even the plots and construction of insane, death-laden operas (which he likened to science fiction) were scrutinized by the young reader.

"After college Tim was drafted into the Army for the Korean War," his sister Patsy recalls. "He was stationed in Fort Dix, New Jersey, Ft. Benning, Georgia, and Arlington, Virginia where he became a cadre (involved in training other troops)." What overshadowed all else during this time was his health; he contracted G.B.S. (Guillain-Barré Syndrome), which, according to the GBS Foundation, is "an inflammatory disorder of the peripheral nerves, those outside the brain and spinal cord. It is characterized by the rapid onset of weakness and, often, paralysis of the legs, arms, breathing muscles and face. GBS is the most common cause of rapidly acquired paralysis in the United States today, affecting one to two people in every 100,000." There is still no cure for it.

Tim spent months at the Walter Reed Hospital in Washington D.C., in bed and in misery. As he told a friend at the time, "At first I was afraid I'd die … Later,

I was afraid I wouldn't." Tim considered the hospital a pest hole and knew that the Army didn't really seem to believe there was such a thing as GBS. For the rest of his life, he was to receive a disability pension because of the damage done to him.

Tim never talked about the Korean War in later life —it was too painful a memory for him. He didn't believe in the war and was uncomfortable with Army life. He hated the authority over him, his creative juices totally suppressed.

Better times were coming.

Chapter
Two

After his Army discharge, Tim was teaching drama in a New Rochelle, New York high school, and four months later, on October 4, 1957, he met his life-long partner, Roland H. Bibolet.

Roland explains: "It was in a gay bar, the Seven Seas, in downtown Phoenix, Arizona. We spent the night at my apartment. We saw a lot of each other for the ensuing weeks, which wasn't easy considering the pressures and demands of our time. Tim had only been in Arizona since July, so as Arizona was 'home' to me, we spent a lot of time going around the state: Mexico, Sedona, Tucson, Grand Canyon, etc., etc.

"I think we were pretty committed after a month or so. I never thought of us as 'soul-mates.' We were actually very different — Boston vs. Southwest, theatre vs. government, floodlights and limelight vs. the back room. We thought of each other as partners, and always introduced each other as 'my buddy,' and Tim usually referred to me as 'my collaborator.' I think one of our strengths was in our differences."

Tim was by then teaching drama in West High in Phoenix; Roland was serving as Administration Assistant to Governor

With Roland, the summer Tim arrived in Phoenix, 1957.

E. W. McFarland. Roland, born in Eagle Pass, Texas on August 31, 1920, was an ensign in the Navy during World War II, and from 1953 to 1955 served as administrative assistant to then Senator Lyndon B. Johnson. He was AA to Arizona Governor Ernest W. McFarland from 1955 to 1958 and program director of KTVK ABC-TV from 1960 to 1964. The blend of politics and showbiz made them a perfect match.

"Tim could deal with urban, urbane, sophisticated people in his writings or rural ranch cowboys!" says Roland.

As for Tim's feelings about his adopted city: "He liked it all but the heat," Roland explained. "That absolutely destroyed him in Phoenix. He lived there from 1957 to 1959 and 1961 to 1964 and then never really went back to the East coast except to visit or attend a Tim Kelly opening. Except for the heat, he was busy writing, directing, working and learning to ride his horse, Popcorn.

"Tim began his writing work, with me helping a *lot*, around 1958. Worked, worked, worked. Tried newspaper work, writing books, articles, stage, radio, TV.

Many times we were almost ready to pack it in. Not until 1995 did our efforts begin to pay off. We did make enough to live on from 1964-1995, just enough to get by, buy a house and travel.

"Tim's first production out West was a Christmas production of *Amhal and the Night Visitors*. He was also acting with the Scottsdale Players and directing and acting in the Phoenix Little Theatre. My life was impossible. The 1958

Above: *Phoenix, circa 1958. Tim & Roland at a reception for Harry Truman.* Left: *Tim, Roland, Buddy & Cissy at home in Phoenix, circa 1964.*

election (which we lost) and starting a new job were traumatic, to say the least."

That was the year Tim took work doing public relations for the Salt River Waters Association, a very big place, since almost all the water in Phoenix is irrigated from man-made lakes high in the mountains to the east and north of the city. Tim would write press releases, pamphlets and brochures, give the occasional Rotary Club-type speech, and do publicity for the company.

He hadn't been in Phoenix long before he began writing theatre reviews for the *Arizona Republic*, the *Phoenix Gazette*, and the *Scottsdale Progress*.

As Roland recalled, "My recollection is that Tim wrote theatre reviews off and on the entire time he lived in Phoenix. My very poor recollection is that he was paid $25 a review. I went to a lot of theatre with Tim, but it was mostly when they were casting one of his plays, when he had a part in the play or when we were involved somehow. In Phoenix, it wasn't far from the Phoenix Little Theatre to the *Arizona Republic* building. He would usually rush over to the paper after the final curtain, type up his story in time for the morning paper. Of course his writing was touched by his being a writer — I think in his case it was a big plus. I've heard him say many times, 'If you don't like the production and the actors are no good, talk about the play, the author, the history of the thing.'"

Tim soon became drama critic for the *Arizona Republic*, and writer for *Arizona Highways* magazine and *Phoenix Point West*.

Trying to branch out, Tim tackled the world of prose with several books, most of which went unpublished. *Paint Me a Murder* was one, originally written under his favorite, most-used pseudonym of Vera S. Morris around 1958. Though

June 10, 1961, San Rafael Church, Ibiza. Vera Morris, Freddie Picard and Roland Bibolet.

in novel format, the entire book was almost all dialogue. Even on the printed page, he was forever the *dramatist*, always thinking "verbally." He later renamed it as *The Museum Murders* (now published by BearManor Media).

Sinners of Ibiza was another of Kelly's novels, written around 1960 after Tim and Roland spent a year in Ibiza, Spain. While there, they met Vera Morris, who was immortalized as the heroine of *Sinners*. Ibiza, Majorca's small sister island, was about 50 miles east of the coast of Spain and known for its non-stop nightlife. Casinos, nude beaches, and a growing youth scene and rise in crime eventually lost Ibiza its touristy luster, but when Tim lived there, it was a vacation setting. He and Roland kept a notebook/sketchbook (95% by Roland) of their time there, some of which was incorporated into the novel. One page listed:

> *gen ideas*
> *Ibiza – Island of the Dogs*
> *They are good to their horses*

chickens run wild
beautiful (but in season only) vegetables:
cabbage
cauliflower
cucumbers
artichokes
peas
lettuce, chard, endive
tomatoes
Fruits in season
citrus
apples poor
grapes
cherries
bananas (Africa)
Spanish tobacco
Chocolate good, from Africa
The music out our window at 3 a.m. – 6 men, a guitar, hand
clapping, etc. and the Anglo yelling to get some sleep
gals on bicycles
2 men on bicycle — one singing
The custom of making a noise outside, in place of knocking
good: chocolate, canned tuna fish, sunglasses
Tailor good but cloth terrible

Tim Kelly in Ibiza, Spain, circa 1960.

Gibraltar, 1960. Returning from their two years in Spain.

"Spain just happened," says Roland. "Tim was at loose ends in Phoenix. I was employed by the *Arizona Highways* Dept. (now ADOT) in 1959. We decided to pack it in and go to Europe for as long as the money lasted. We quit our jobs, rented the Phoenix house, drove to Boston-New York City, and sailed in August aboard the *Oslofjord* to Oslo. Then by train through Norway, Sweden, Denmark, West Germany, the Netherlands, Belgium, France to Spain by October; then Barcelona and Palma de Majorca. Tim came down with hepatitis for a month and during his convalescence we heard about Ibiza about 100 miles from Palma. So, we went overnight by ship and it was so cheap we could even afford it!

"We stayed a week in a pension and rented a house for the rest of the time we were there. We bought a portable typewriter — I think I still have it in Hollywood — in Barcelona and yes, Tim wrote every day. He worked mostly on *From the Ashes*, his unpublished novel about Phoenix, and began *Sinners of Ibiza*, his unpublished novel about Ibiza. It was a primitive place — it took two electricians three visits to get him a working floor lamp — but it was warm, quiet and cheap. We lived an idyllic year there. He also did some articles for *Arizona Highways* and *Phoenix Point West* there."

Even on vacation, Tim's work ethic was strong. He was always looking for characters, and Roland proved to be a willing "Watson" to Tim's " Sherlock Holmes." In the following notes, Roland's aptitude for descriptive writing is evident.

Beach Personalities

Germans — noisy, most active. Long-striped bathrobes, heavy set, healthy, enjoying everything, beachwear out of 1930s. Come early, stay late. Much beach gear: mattresses, towels, balls, boats, cars, trailers.

French — Strip down to postage stamp and enjoy the sun – most youthful acting.

English — Come dressed "formal," lift up their shirts above knees and sit in beach chairs. Seldom have hats or cover head with beach towel or handkerchief. They sound funny to us.

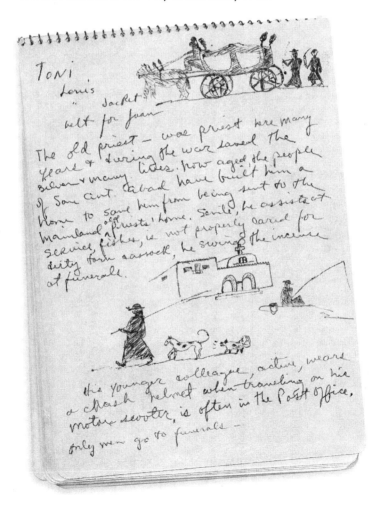

Beats — Walk to beach, sit on rock and write or read. They should bring soap.

Spanish — The maid brings the kids at 9. At 11 Mama comes with 3 hampers and 4 visiting aunts. The kids are slinging sand when Papa arrives at 2, suited, and tries to sit and eat. He brings a business associate and they argue over the decimal point. SOP: call the attendant every 3 minutes to move the beach chairs.

Ibicencans — No women. The boys swim in old bathing suits or jockey shorts and spend most of their time walking past and calling to the "chicas." Rove in packs, aged 4 to 80, looking for exposed female flesh, get kicks from women changing.

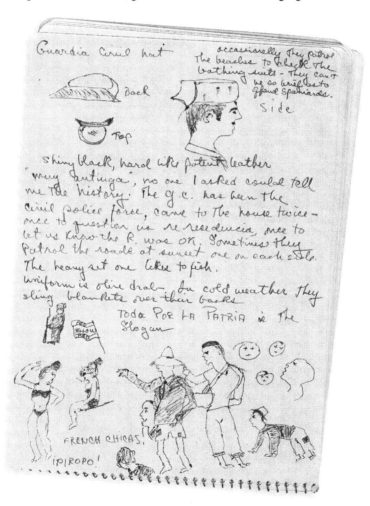

People — 1. Ibicencan 2. Spanish 3. English 4. Beats 5. Germans 6. French 7. Dutch

Misc. — 1. gunnel (Swede) 2. American 3. clergy 4. dogs 5. moors. 6. Formenteran

Roland also took notes on specific people who would soon become Kelly characters:

Pepa — spinster. All her family women are "short." She makes a good living at 10 pesetas an hour (14 cents) on her knees. Super-stitious churchgoer, tells if laundry's done by the "sniff" method, said never use hot water when washing glasses. Loves flowers. Stands about 4'10," never married because her tongue is too sharp, arranged for Margarita and "lorded" it over her. Never would eat with us, chocolate bocadillo, gave us cheese and mushroom spread because it was too sharp for her. Loves Moorish music on radio given her.

Chapter Three

Ninety fifty-eight was Tim's breakout year as a playwright. Gene Dingenary produced his *A Darker Flower* for the Pocket Theatre in New York City. Four years later Harper & Row published his first stage mystery, *Widow's Walk* (see Appendix for synopsis); the same year his *A Darker Flower* opened in New York, *The Trunk and All That Jazz* opened in Boston, and *Die Blum* premiered in Germany. The first of his many published plays from Sam French came in 1964 with *King of the Golden River*.

Left: *Tim at Yale, 1964.* Right: *Roland & Tim at home in Hollywood, circa 1965.*

From there, his drama took off dramatically.

Tim was off to Yale. He had won a TV drama contest, in which winning writers received a workshop at Yale from September 1964 to June 1965. It was a joint ABC/KTVK contest for which about twenty people across the country were admitted. Tim went not as a writer or teacher but as a dramatist. The course was oriented to Hollywood scriptwriting.

Roland recalled: "When he was named as one of the ABC contest winners, Tim quit his job at Salt River and I quit my job as program director of KTVK. The view in mind was for Tim to attend the class and for me to hold the homestead fort there. We took our dog Buddy and our cat Sabbatha and all lived in Candlewood Isle, Connecticut."

One week after the Yale course ended, Tim was in Hollywood. He flew out, followed four months later in a Volkswagon by Roland, Buddy and Sabbatha. The seeds of writing for TV and film were sewn, but it was Arizona that kept Tim active in the medium he loved most dearly: The Theatre.

Tim's sister, Patsy: "Mother went to visit Tim in Phoenix around 1962, and at that time he was the drama critic for the *Arizona Republic* newspaper. Before they went out to dinner and a play that evening, Tim handed mother a stack of letters and said, 'Here, read some of these.' Ma said they were awful — people criticizing Tim's opinions of the dramas and she said to him, 'Don't these nasty letters bother you?' He answered, 'No — I would be more bothered if I didn't get these letters. This way, by getting the letters, I know that people are reading what I write.'"

Strong community ties were paying off. He was starting to get his plays produced.

Tim, extreme left, at Yale University.

The January 30, 1964 edition of *The Arizonian* lauded the strong relationship between The Scottsdale Players and "one of the Valley's most talented and prolific young writers, Tim Kelly." On February 7th his *Song of the Dove* was set to open, featuring John Greenslade and Royce Weyers in the cast. The Scottsdale Players had previously produced two of his mysteries, *The Burning Man*, and the world premiere of *Widow's Walk*, plus the three-act children's play, *King of the Golden River*.

"Community theatres — and the Scottsdale Players are that in the best sense of the word — perform a great service for playwrights," Kelly told *The Arizonian*. "The adage that plays are not written but rewritten is very true. Only when he sees his play performed on stage does it really come alive for the writer. He sees it in perspective for the first time. During the first week of rehearsals for *Song of the Dove*, I cut it by forty-five minutes."

The production got a lot of local press before it premiered on February 7th at the Stagebrush Theatre in the Scottsdale Community Center performed by the Scottsdale Players. It played two additional weekends and the play was excerpted in *Phoenix Point West*. Tim explained, "I personally consider their narrative one of history's real love stories, one that has never received its just due. To the list of Antony and Cleopatra, Rudolf and Marie of Mayerling —

Tim, Roland and friend, Clyde Senger in Candlewood Isle, Connecticut (while at Yale, 1964). Buddy's in the background.

even our old friends Romeo and Juliet — I place the names of Maximilian and Carlota. Walking through Vienna a few years ago, I was taken by the city's fantastic contrast to the Mexico I knew. Yet Vienna and Mexico City during the American Civil War were allied through the personages of the young Emperor and his barren, high-strung wife."

The literate, romantic drama told the tragic story of these young monarchs, weaving pertinent history into the play and touching upon the founding of the French Foreign Legion (a corps created to serve an Austrian emperor in North America), Louis-Napoleon's duplicity, the Monroe Doctrine, and the rise of Mexican nationalism.

A voracious appetite for reading fueled this attention to historic detail in Tim's period pieces. Every book, article and footnote he read eventually wound up in his writings.

"I think I was closer to Tim than anyone," states Roland. "He was almost W.C. Fieldsian in playing his cards close [to the vest] and in not fully trusting anyone. But mainly, he kept to himself so he could *write*, freely, as he needed to and on his own schedule. I never knew him to miss a deadline."

"Writing was his life. His muse was always in control. Sometimes I would be awakened at 3 or 4 a.m. by the *tap! tap! tap!* of his machine. He always had several ideas going."

A typical day would have Tim rising between 9:30 to 10:30, going down for coffee at Schwab's Drug Store, and returning about noon to start work around 1 p.m. He worked until 6, 7 or 8, with time out for dinner. These were the times there were no appointments, no presentations and no "working" lunches.

His agent thought he had too many ideas going to keep them all under one name. Some readers and producers wouldn't believe all of this was coming from the same writer. But there was a more important reason for grabbing several pen names: Tim knew that producers and movie executives loved to pigeonhole talent, refusing to believe that one person could successfully write in several genres. It had happened during his stint on *High Chaparral*; no one believed he was capable of anything other than western scripts. Play producers were the same. In 1991 Tim told *Drama-Logue*, "All of the commercial playwrights that I know write under more than one name and write more than one kind of play."

Mystery, melodrama, comedy — he liked writing them all.

Road Show birthed the following headline: "Tim J. Kelly's Road Show Farce Ridiculously Funny, Critic Says." The review from Anson B. Cutts in Phoenix's newspaper on July 8, 1959 read: "Last night at Phoenix Little Theatre, Phoenicians witness for the third time within a year a new play by a Valley author.

"The action, which is singularly innocent of motivation, takes place in a high class theatrical boarding house in Hershey, PA, upon which descends an old-time stage star, Jennie Flagg, who has seen better days and is touring in "The First Mrs. Fraser." In her retinue is her juvenile, a too, too precious young actor, and Baby, her pet toy poodle. Both require more coddling than all of the people in the house put together.

"These include a young playwright, Warren Henderson, who turns out to be the unloved son of Jennie, and whose wife is starring in his latest ill-fated play, with considerable strain on the family ties, plus a long-suffering landlady, whose teenage daughter is stage-struck; and a gamut of other assorted characters.

"Paula Sobol, playing Jennie, made the actress a personality long to be remembered, thanks to her slick comic flair, a voice that only an actor could love, and costumes that made her look like Superman garlanded with diamonds. Grace Etchen turned in a very smooth, believable performance as the harassed housekeeper and mother, Mrs. Knudson.

"Her daughter, Lillian, as played by Susan Francis, was a bit too eager and automatic at the beginning, but her scene, as the siren who nails the juvenile on the sofa, was one of the funniest in the play. Two crotchety old biddies were played to the hilt by Irma Lange and Betty Turner. Outstanding male performance was that by Bill Van Loo, as the effete juvenile actor, Bobby, who gets very, very drunk toward the end."

But even community theatre could be a difficult sale. The following article written for Tim's "One on the Aisle" column (usually containing his theatre reviews) from *The Arizonian* on May 22, 1960 could have been written today, with little theatres now putting on mostly "known" properties.

In the 20's the American theatre had become so thoroughly commercialized that it became almost impossible to pick more than a handful of works from any season that amounted to anything worthwhile. Happy at the end of World War I, playgoers settled for a lumpy bowl of theatrical porridge. Plays as watery as the worst of the Clyde Fitch soap operas prospered. It was a period in which a dramatist with any ideas might just as well have settled in Paris (which many of them did), where tiny theatres would give his work a looksee if it had merit. Appalled by the steady variation on the "Pollyanna Theme" displayed on the commercial stages of New York, the "Little Theatre Movement" was born.

Its purpose was to abandon the going-nowhere trends of Broadway and present plays that took an audience's intelligence for granted. Eugene O'Neil began his career this way. No Broadway producer would gamble with his work, but a hard core of people interested in Theatre would, and they did. They performed the works in an old warehouse in Provincetown, Massachusetts. In the daytime they tripped over fishnets and oars. At night they opened the rear of the warehouse to the sea and before this background performed gems like *Ile, In the Zone, Bound East for Cardiff* and the first draft of *Marco's Millions*. In the winter they journeyed to Washington Square in downtown Manhattan and became the Washington Players; later a segment of this group became the core of the Theatre Guild.

The "Little Theatre Movement" began in anarchy and lives, today, in almost rigid conformity to Broadway hitism, begging that it be allowed inadequately to copy whatever Broadway offered last season.

The Off-Broadway movement, which now has in operation more theatres than does Broadway, produces only those plays that Broadway will not accept because it fears financial (not artistic) failure. Plays that flopped (financially) on the uptown stages like *The Crucible, Children of Darkness, The Threepenny Opera, The Iceman Cometh, A Clearing in the Woods* and *Take a Giant Step* (to mention but a few of the contemporary works) were all unhappy events uptown, but roaring successes when produced with an eye to artistic rather than financial success in the small theatres with "low overhead." The list of European and classical dramatists whose works are represented each season off-Broadway is staggering.

Unfortunately, only the commercial Broadway trends reach Phoenix. Only plays that have been "hits" are usually considered for production. Good plays that fail financially are deemed failures all around. Unpleasant plays are deemed "unpleasant" from every aspect. And occasionally, when someone comes up with an idea for experimentation, it is the offbeatness of a bygone and proven age. (One Phoenix group is even contemplating offering as an experimental work Ibsen's *A Doll's House*, which in this day and age is about as experimental as producing *Bambi* in the children's reading room at the Public Library. *A Doll's House* even in its own age was daring only in theme, not in manner of direction, design, acting, style or form.)

Plays that are vigorous, challenging; asking an audience to think, argue, question or protest are deemed, in most cases, wholly unsuitable for production. The Valley playhouse that can technically perform the classics will not. The Greek dramatists are ignored, the Restoration Period Plays overlooked, the European playwrights and dramatists shunned. Musical theatre, the only contribution America has given world theatre in concept, style and form, is relegated to an "also ran" status and, in some cases, ignored completely because it's "too much trouble." So what's left? A soggy patty-cake of entertainment yeast that never rises.

The one theatre that struggles to present what the others will not is the Stagebrush Theatre here in Scottsdale, but it is handicapped by physical limitations. Still, in one season of playgoing at the Stagebrush Theatre, a playgoer can make the acquaintance of some very interesting writers and plays.

The Valley's potential for creating its "own" theatre, independent of Broadway's commercialism, is boundless. The opportunity heeded to create something fine, similar to what Margo Jones had in Dallas, exists here in the Valley. But it would seem that the "Little Theatre Movement" has washed its hands and now sits stiffly, self-righteously, in its well-scrubbed pew.

It was Emerson, I believe, who said: "Yesterday's radical is today's conservative."

At best, it is an embarrassing situation in which THEATRE finds itself.

Chapter
Four

From 1965 until the year he died, Tim was living in Hollywood. In June of that year he and Roland rented a house off Laurel Canyon.

"We lived there," said Roland, "until we found, bought and moved to the house on Lookout Mountain Ave. They are only two or three miles apart. The area is very mountainous. Both addresses were located very conveniently for our purposes."

Their house was about five minutes from the Sunset Strip, ten minutes from the San Fernando Valley (Studio City, California), fifteen minutes from Hollywood Blvd. & Vine, fifteen minutes from Paramount, half an hour from Universal and Warner Bros. studios, an hour from Culver City (MGM), and ninety minutes from the Los Angeles airport.

From there, he wrote even more. His brief ride as a published novelist culminated in his biggest success: *Ride of Fury*. "New blood for old massacres" as the first page teaser stated; "It was known as Miller's Massacre — two dead, two carried off by the Apaches, and one survivor. Now the boy had grown to manhood and he had never lost his conviction that his sisters could be found.

At home in Hollywood, circa 1965.

"Cos Fury was hired for the job. A man who had fought and loved the desert all his life, the Apaches had taken something from him, too — an auburn-haired girl he had loved. In her picture in the locket, Ann Miller had auburn hair too.

"So he rode, against the heat of the desert, against the violence of the Apaches, against all odds, to follow the rumors of a white 'Squaw Virgin' held by the Indians."

Published as an Ace Double (flip the paperback over for a second complete novel) in 1964, the 45-cent handheld paperback sported a typical pulp western cover with a scared black horse and a steady gunslinger ready for action.

The Arizona Republic gave *Ride of Fury* a good review: "Authentic in Southwestern detail as might be expected from him, Kelly's book about an Apache massacre and the surviving son who sets out to find his captive sister, is quick-moving.

"The survivor hires a professional hunter of humans, Cos Fury, and it is Fury's story as he struggles against the desert, Apache violence and Army ineptitude to find the girl.

"The book itself is unusual in makeup. Held one way it features Kelly's story, reverse the book and a second novel, *The Blind Trail* by Reese Sullivan, is uppermost. Two action Westerns for the price of one."

Incidentally, the name "Fury" derived from Tim's maternal grandfather, Furey.

Though later jeered by critics at large, in 1967 they were paying attention to Tim Kelly's plays. *Late Blooming Flowers* (original title: *Does the Sun Always Shine in the South of France?*), based on the novel by Chekhov about the trials of poor Russian royalty, gathered the following pre-Broadway reviews.

The Los Angeles Times: "Kelly has caught both Chekhov's essence of people drowning unaware in quicksand and the humor of the great writer... he skillfully catches the flavor, the depth of characterization and the poignant mood of the Russian Master."

Citizen-News: "The effect is startling — as if an apprentice painter had lovingly completed an unfinished Rembrandt."

The Hollywood Reporter: "...a moving and illuminating experience."

Roland remembered "being at casting rehearsals and opening nights for *Welcome to the Casa* and *Late Blooming*. There were cast parties and constant dialogue changes. And I remember this incredibly fat woman reading for a part in *Flowers*. She made the boards groan."

Tim's original *Welcome to the Casa* also caught the eye of *Citizen-News*: "...a literate drama...holds attention as well as promise. Kelly's feeling for form, character and dialogue align him with those playwrights who write well-made plays, draw their people with care and communicate their intentions in words that make sense and stir up excitement."

It was also Roland's favorite play.

"Perhaps I am selfish because of all his plays, that one comes closest to me," he admits. "I grew up in the area, knew the characters and supplied the Mexican,

Western cowboy and local nomenclature and feel. My second favorite would be *Everything's Jim Dandy*, for exactly the same reasons."

In the late 1960s Tim was also having great success at writing for television. (Even though he came to Hollywood in May 1966 and didn't sell his first work until November 1968.) One of his highest-profile series was *The High Chaparral*, which ran from 1967 to 1971. Taking place at the High Chaparral Ranch in 1870s' Arizona Territory, it was an intelligent western that dealt with the trials the Cannon family had of bordering the Apaches and Mexicans while still trying to grow their cattle business into an empire. It was created by David Dortort, who scored a huge success with *Bonanza*.

Tim, Buddy & Pal in the Hollywood house, 1968.

Roland explained the rigors of a television writer: "Tim wrote over twenty-five episodes of *High Chaparral* and I suppose I helped a bit on each one. Our usual pattern was 1) endless talking over a new idea for a script; the idea came from either or both of us, or was an assignment; 2) getting some sort of outline by both of us; 3) typing it into a story, usually by Tim; 4) scene-by-scene by Tim, with a line-by-line go-over as it came out of the typewriter by both of us; 5) proofing, usually by me. Then it went to the typist and submission. Somewhere along this trail we usually had some differences of opinion. Tim won most arguments.

"As time went on, as Tim became more sure and more able, my influence, my role became less and less. He almost always talked to me and sent me the script before submission.

"His agents (Jack Stewart mostly) would set him up with the production staff of various TV shows — *High Chaparral, Bonanza, Name of the Game, Those Were the Days, Nakia* — the list is endless. Tim would bring in a 'story' and then *if accepted*, the poor guy went through a multitude of rewrite steps. I felt there were rewrites sometimes *because* they were provided for. If *not* accepted, the whole thing died — after long waits. That was really hard on Tim.

"Most writing for film or TV is boring and tedious. Everything is a battle. Here is an example: In an episode of *High Chaparral*, the plot hinged on a telegram. The historical wire arrived in Arizona some ten years after this episode, but when we pointed this out to the director, his rejoinder was, 'Don't bother me with facts!'"

Still, it was a heady experience to be a television writer. He even got a few bit parts as an actor, just for the experience.

Patsy recalled, "One day we were told to watch the television series *26 Men*. He landed a bit part by telling them he knew how to ride a horse. Got on the horse and fell off. They gave him another role. He told us the date as to when it would be shown on TV. We were ready, heads glued to the TV screen and pointer sticks with which to point him out in case he was in the background. The pro-gram started, the rider on the horse coming up to the water trough where a man was wash-ing his face. The rider spoke to the man, the man turned around, and there was Tim — the man who was washing his face — a beautiful close-up of him filling our 21" TV screen. He had a small speaking part before he was hit over the head and fell down, but for us it sure was a sight to see!"

Above: *The Lookout Mt. Ave. house, circa 1969.* Below: *Their first home in Hollywood on Walnut Drive. Roland is on the balcony.*

Roland states, "Until 1983, when it became necessary for me to spend more time in Ari-zona, he and I discussed almost everything he worked on — movies, plays, TV, and the book. Where I was most help-ful and creative was with stuff dealing with the West, cowboys, Mexico. The way people talk about brands, cattle, ranching."

His newfound success meant more income. But as Tom Owen, Tim's tax man from 1970, recalled, "Tim was really tight with money. He trusted no one but the bank, and had accounts in a lot of them. He kept detailed records in little books and on funny schedules. I tried many times to get him to invest in different things but he always said no. The only thing he did was have a retirement plan that he invested all of the profits of the cor-poration in. The corporation and the retirement plan were only in effect to lessen his income tax burden. He made them both very legal and I'm sure drove everyone nuts with 'what if' questions. In the end he paid a lot to the IRS, which he didn't like at *all.*

"He was a true Democrat and 'knew' that all Republicans were crazy. He was a very deep thinker who could talk on many subjects. He liked solitude and routine, welcomed invited guests and didn't like surprises. He really liked the house on Lookout Mountain Avenue — it was quiet and secluded."

Roland clarifies that "Tim was *not* tight with money, but [he was] *secretive* about it. He did have about a dozen accounts scattered around southern California, which kept me scurrying about for a while."

Chapter Five

As time went on and Tim's output increased at such an exponential rate, this playwrighting machine was forced to adopt more pen names to allow drama directors the choice of author, rather than simply reading from the "Tim Kelly Catalog" (which is what they were doing anyway), such as some of Pioneer's catalogs seemed to be. Keith Jackson, Robert Swift, Vera Morris, J. Moriarty (Sherlock Holmes' nemesis) and Roland Bibolet were a few of the word-disguises within which he cloaked his prolificity. He continued to write for six hours a day, six days a week, religiously.

Vera Morris, 1969. Ibiza, Spain.

Roland stated that "Tim worried about being too prolific, but that didn't slow down his output. As you have noticed, some of the catalogues have been almost all 'Tim Kelly' listings. That's why he used so many names, like Vera Morris, etc. He wanted to have at least one play in every play publishing publication, and he loved entering contests. He told me his output would slow when he reached sixty-two-and-a-half — it didn't. He ended his life writing plays and had a backlog of projects when he died."

Tim's prolificity was later recognized in the British magazine *Million* (*The Magazine About Popular Fiction*) by author Brad Spurgeon. In the article, Lope de Vega, with 1,800 plays and 400 religious pieces, was quoted as history's champion prolific playwright; but Tim was easily listed as today's most *produced*. Other hard workers included romance novelist Barbara Cartland who, at the advanced age of 90, was still going strong even after 507 books, with half a billion copies sold. Sci-fi writers Robert Silverberg & Isaac Asimov, textbook writer Ronald Ridout (515 textbooks written), and novelist Eleanor Hibbert were also singled out for their amazing ability to sit in one place for hours at a time.

Tim always had plans for plays — every event, every piece of scenery was dramatic to him. Most of his ideas came from his own head, reading (loads of adaptations came out of this) or, when he was established, suggestions from his publishers.

Roland recalled one fleeting inspiration: "One of his plays is called *Masha*, simply because he said 'Marcia' with a Boston accent, and I didn't see it until it was accepted. I had suggested the name to him earlier. I have a niece named Marcia and we both liked it.

"During his last eight years he had developed his style and was so popular he didn't need much help.

"There is a pattern to his high-school-oriented stuff:

"1. an institution — a school, a hotel, a big old house

"2. a dowager type

"3. a housekeeper

"4. a handyman

"5. teenagers, family members, love interest

"6. a financial problem

"7. a detective, reporter, police officer

"8. a mysterious stranger

"He used all of these very theatrically, very well and very differently — [it was] part of his genius. The measure of his independence: the last thing out of his typewriter — the thing about the '20s, called, I believe, *Flapper*. I had never heard of it till the typist brought it to me posthumously!"

His high rate of performance and publication also stemmed from knowing what kinds of plays schools were seeking: G-rated, usually one-set, large casts for its group to dig into, with more women than men (since women audition for the theatre more frequently than men). His success became almost mainstream in its elitism, so much so that *Writer's Digest* had him pen "How to Write and Sell the Play" for their May 1977 issue (now reprinted as part of *Forget Broadway — How to Get 3 Plays Produced in a Year* by Tim Kelly).

"A great deal of *my* day," says Roland, "was spent in taking and picking up scripts from Barbara's Place, or Ann Block, or Mimi O'Graph's [typists]. It was expensive, time-consuming and cumbersome, but that's how it had to be. The scripts for submission by Tim Kelly were clean, had *wonderful* covers and were useable by the receiver! I have stacks of them in the garage. After a play was in print, I would use these copies for scratch pads and letter writing. When Tim noted this he was *furious* and I stopped it. Sort of like using the Good Book in the outhouse!"

When musicals were required, the publishers, especially Pioneer Drama, simply handed over his scripts to a composer for adaptation. Songwriter Bill Francoeur put songs to nine of his plays before ever meeting the playwright. Tim would be specific about what he wanted, in terms of emotional tone and musical styles. Bill was possibly the best collaborator Tim ever had in the musical part of his life. The two had a connection.

For *Kilroy Was Here*, Tim included suggested songs and a floor plan along with the manuscript, and stated, "Although film musicals covered the WWII period fairly well, there is 'almost' nothing from the stage. So, we have a pretty clear field. As always, if you make any changes for musical reasons (including song titles) do make the required alteration(s) in the text. Should prove a great deal of fun for a youthful cast."

Tim knew that the key to being a successful playwright in the school market was to give them what they wanted. As he wrote to Bill on October 18, 1997: "Enclosed copy of *GROOVY!* Eight songs. As always, make any necessary text changes needed to accommodate your lyrics. For the obvious reasons much of

TIM KELLY
8730 LOOKOUT MOUNTAIN AVE.
HOLLYWOOD, CALIFORNIA 90046
(213) 656-9453

STAGE MURDER, MAYHEM & MYSTERY

29 October 1991

Bill Francoeur
555 West Dillon Road
Louisville, Colorado 80027

RE: WAGON WHEELS WEST

Dear Bill:

Enclosed acting version/book for WAGON WHEELS WEST.

I have indicated where the songs should come and what they
should be 'about'. And I have given each selection a song
title. However, feel free to go for a different title(s)
if it would work better musically. Who sings what is indicated.

The only 'plot' gimmick is the repeating of the phrase
'Anything Can Happen' so, maybe, it's important to keep
that title. Or, the 'gimmick' can simply be blue-pencilled.

Make any minor changes direct to PIONEER. I have mailed
on a c. to Steve & Sheila.

Any hassles let me know, but musically I'll leave it to
you. Should prove a winner.

Best,

Tim K.

Tim K.
Encls.

21 August 1992

Dear Bill:

Enclosed synopsis for YOU AIN'T NOTHING BUT A WEREWOLF.

With all the hoopla from A.I.P. about the remake of the Michael
Landon 'classic' and the slew of werewolf (teenage) flicks on
the production slates here in Hollywood this should prove not
only a heap of fun but quite profitable, too.

Anyway, the synopsis will give you a good idea of what the
completed script will be - and I hope to have the completed
script to you/Pioneer 'bout Thanksgiving time.

Keep in touch.

Tim

ref./encl. YOU AIN'T NOTHIN' BUT A WEREWOLF

8730 LOOKOUT MOUNTAIN AVENUE ● HOLLYWOOD, CALIFORNIA 90046 ● (213) 656-9453

the 60's stuff is glossed over or ignored — Vietnam, Civil Rights Movements, Cold War, Cuban Missiles, blah, blah, blah. All it takes to lose a production is for one teacher or parent to object to 'something.' *GROOVY!*, thus, is a light entertainment for a young cast and audience. A money-making (hopefully) 'show.' I surely did want to toss in a number called 'Tune In, Turn On, Drop Out' and another 'Make Love, Not War' but sanity prevailed. Thankfully."

After hearing Bill's score, Tim wrote, "Played *GROOVY!* several times and,

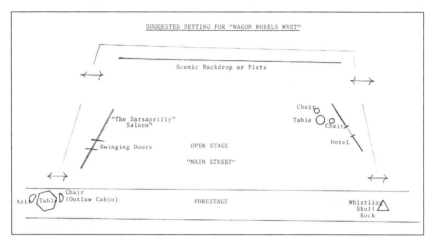

Tim's suggested floorplan for Wagon Wheels West *sent to Bill Francoeur.*

yes, you're right. It's going to be a winner. The kids will love doing it. Your score really captures the era (and I lived thru it)! That opening sitar music is a stroke of genius."

"Tim was the most un-musical person I ever knew," admits Roland. "He described himself as stone deaf. In his early works I supplied any poetry he needed, such as the song in *King of the Golden River*. Later, he had musical talent (Bill Francoeur, etc.). Tim always kept creative control. He would tell Bill what the scene, dialogue and situation was and sometimes suggested the words needed.

"Strange, he loved music. Once when the Met was doing *La Boheme*, he called me (Los Angeles to Arizona) and we listened to the second act together over the phone.

"He loved opera and went when he could. He lived through the entire *Ring* cycle in Seattle in the '70s, and we went to several 'zarzuelas' in Madrid, but musicals on Broadway were his first love. He had hundreds of albums (the old 78s) and he had something on — full-blast — most of the time he was at his typewriter. *Man of La Mancha, Oklahoma, South Pacific, Guys & Dolls* come to mind. My recollection is that he would write scene by scene in great silence, and then music for the corrections, rewrites, blue pencils, cutting and pasting, spelling stuff (both Tim and I have no spelling skills), and getting the script in shape for the typist.

"Sadly, as Tim grew in experience, ability and fame, he closed in. His study in Hollywood has windows on three sides and we had to swatch them in heavily-lined zarapes, which he kept tightly closed all the time. Every window in the house could be closed, therefore. A very efficient air conditioning system kept the temperature where he wanted it. Even the bedroom windows let in no moonlight.

"He hated interruptions — telephone calls were destructive. When he was 'into' something, we had an arrangement: I cooked and he said, 'I can break at 7:30 p.m.' At 7:10 I would say, 'Dinner in 20 minutes.' He could live with that system. His creativity was a cruel master. I've seen him interrupt watching TV, reading, conversation with guests at dinner, even sleep, to slink out to his desk for five minutes of typing."

Chapter Six

Tim Kelly was busy writing for the stage and television, but the transition from television to film writing was inevitable.

Tim's most successful motion picture was probably 1970's *Cry of the Banshee*. This low-budget American International Productions' gothic witchcraft melodrama starred Vincent Price, which gave it an almost-instant immortality. The most interesting part of the film perhaps came from the opening animated titles provided by then-*Monty Python* member, Terry Gilliam. Released on

Vincent Price in Cry of the Banshee, 1970.

July 22nd, the film was supposedly shot in the one-time mansion of W.S. Gilbert in Middlesex, England.

Strangely, director Gordon Hessler did not mention Tim at all in his on-screen interview as a Special Feature on the DVD release. But according to Hessler, the first script of *Banshee* was so bad that he and friend Christopher Wicking ("additional dialogue" on Hessler's *The Oblong Box*, and later, *Murders in the Rue Morgue*) had to do extensive rewrites. Not only did this action take the film further away from its original meaning & script, but it became more of an exploitation vehicle, complete with gratuitous nudity and violence. Full of timely, late '60s directing tricks, such as point-of-view shots and emotionally high acting (and not just from the cult group who look stoned anyway), *Cry of the Banshee* did attempt to blend in an old-world style into the performances (particularly effective is the fine stage actress Elisabeth Bergner in the role of Oona, a vengeful sorceress), and the period look of it still holds up today.

Far less effective is the film's eponymous banshee, which occupies only a few seconds of on-screen time. This monster has been likened to "a Halloween party werewolf" with its obvious rubber mask, protruding teeth, and a fright wig of gray hair.

Roland recalled one bit of help he gave Tim on that screenplay: "In one scene the viewer knows a door must be opened. Terrible banging noise. You are just sure a Boris Karloff, an ogre, a dragon is going to be revealed. My suggestion: when the door opens, there is a small child, radiant and beautiful. He bought it and it works beautifully.

Tim adapted the story for the stage as well.

"*Cry of the Banshee* had the biggest star we ever snagged. It's also still going! Once Tim and I bumped shopping carts with Vincent Price in Safeway and Tim didn't even identify himself to Price!"

Like all writers, Tim faced his share of rejection.

Roland states, "Tim *did* write a few things which never moved, especially film scripts. He was like a bulldog about his stuff, never giving up, even when the battle was lost. Artistically for him, a play wasn't completed until it was performed. He used to call his rejected projects 'my ugly daughters' (is a play always female?). He *did* participate in round tables—UCLA, ASU come to mind—and very often they would invite him to be playwright in residence. He loved working with the kids, but this was *always* exhausting for him; he was a very private person. But he was ready to do *anything* to get his stuff going. This resulted in Hollywood— at least, in my opinion—of people taking advantage of him."

It wasn't all scripts for Tim, however. In the early 1970s he wrote for *The Advocate*, a gay magazine.

Roland: "Tim was a liberal democrat and Democrat, a gay libber (he walked in several coast parades) and contributed to several causes. PAWS, a pet rescue operation, was a favorite."

He and Roland had a dream about raising a child.

"Always just one, always a boy," says Roland, "and if we had lived thirty years later, I'm sure it would have happened. I think Tim would have been abrupt with any child who interrupted his work, but he was good, very good with students of theatre. I think Tim and kids clicked in a theatre setting only."

Reporters were most enamored of his prolific output, though Tim was usually careful in differentiating between his two kinds of plays: the commercial ones, and the harder-to-marry-off "ugly" serious works. Because of the intense difficulty of placing those serious plays (which he claimed went mostly to England), "I have to write three commercial plays before I can write a serious play." He did not write for the mental exercise—the point was to have these creations *live*.

"Dramatists are in a peculiar position in today's society," he once said. "We are bow-and-arrow makers in a world of neutron bombs."

Roland stated that Tim's intense drive to keep writing stemmed from growing up in the Great Depression: "Hard work times, poor families. If you want something, work for it'—that was the motto of the times. We both worked our way through college (and before). Also, Tim was *driven* to be a dramatist by everything in him. As to my (much lesser) contribution, I was motivated by love.

"He never went to a movie, watched TV, listened to radio, traveled, even socialized without relating it to whatever he was working on. There was *always* something in the typewriter."

Tim with Digger & Elvis at home, Hollywood, circa 1970.

In 1982 *Drama Logue* reported that Tim was averaging an incredible 5,000 performances annually, in all 50 states and in 12 foreign countries. He was credited as having written 120 western novels over a seven-year period; in fact, *Ride of Fury* was his only one. He also gave his views on the state of Broadway and play-selling in general. He didn't believe that just because a play has a Broadway run that that should be the deciding factor of why certain plays finally find a life outside the catalog while still others might be sitting in the catalog, unproduced, for years.

"Plays I've had published thirty years ago are still being produced," Tim said with obvious pride. "There are New York plays that were hailed by critics and never heard of again."

Chapter
Seven

One of Tim's most celebrated "exploitation" films was a difficult experience for him, as Hollywood shaped it into something he hadn't originally intended for it to be. *Sugar Hill* (1974), with its hip/dated theme song "Supernatural Voodoo Woman," is certainly a cult movie, atmospheric in zombie delight. From the opening strains of its theme song ("Supernatural voodoo woman does her thing at night/Supernatural voodoo woman, do her wrong and you won't see the light") to the final fade-out, it is a horror fantasy like none other.

Below is a detailed article on the film that first appeared in *Midnight Marquee* magazine (issue #55, fall 1997). It is reprinted here with the kind permission of the author.

"Sugar Hill and Her Zombie Hit Men!"
By Bryan Senn

Meet *Sugar Hill*...
it's not a place; it's a brand new face.
She's the hippest chick in town!

"She found all the forces of evil,
Put them in a voodoo trance,
She used all her tools to put the fools away,
And evil never had a chance"

— from the theme song, "Supernatural Voodoo Woman"

The 1970s were something of a cultural wasteland in America, full of bad fashion (polyester leisure suits and voluminous bell-bottoms), bad hair (who can forget the gigantic afro phase?), and bad music (one word: disco). Consequently, a "modern" American movie from the '70s (particularly one that strove for a "hip" contemporary look) is *instantly* recognizable for the cultural curiosity it is.

Though this writer "came of age" during the 1970s, he holds little nostalgic love for it, a personal prejudice perhaps, but one that seems justified when the decade's shortcomings are so bluntly exposed by films like *Sugar Hill*. It's not a bad movie; in fact it possesses a solid story, some moments of effective atmosphere, and decent production values. It's just hopelessly trapped in the thick amber of its time period. The dated dialogue and charmless "jive" talk ("That's a very foxy lady"), the ridiculous she-bop Motown theme song ("Supernatural voodoo woman does her thing at night; Supernatural voodoo woman, do her wrong and you won't see the light"), and the wide lapels on powder blue pant-suits only serve to distract from the tale being told. Consequently, it's sometimes difficult to take seriously. Even so, for those with more tolerance for the sights and sounds of "K-Tel" and the like, *Sugar Hill* offers up a well-produced and often atmospheric tale of voodoo vengeance.

Marki Bey plays Diana "Sugar" Hill, whose lover, a nightclub owner named Langston (Larry D. Johnson), is beaten to death in his club's parking lot by a gang of thugs headed by crime boss Mr. Morgan (Robert Quarry). Thirsting for vengeance, Sugar returns to the old Bayou plantation house where she grew up to seek the aid of Mama Maitresse (Zara Cully), a voodoo witch.

The old sorceress leads Sugar to a secret mist-shrouded grave-yard in the swampland where she calls upon "Baron Samedi, keeper of the dead, king of the graveyards." When the Baron (Don Pedro Colley) appears, Sugar offers him her soul in exchange for his aid, but the voodoo god ("a great lover," cackles Mama Maitresse) lasciviously counters, "It's not your *soul* I want."* Baron Samedi then raises up a band of zombies, the corpses of buried slaves, and instructs Sugar to "put them to *evil* use; it's all they know or want."

In a dockside warehouse, Sugar confronts the first of Morgan's men, Tank (Rick Hagood). "You and your punk friends killed my man," she pronounces, "and the sentence is *death!*"

The zombies descend on him and hack him to death with machetes. Police detective Valentine (Richard Lawson), an old flame of Sugar's, finds a slave shackle near Tank's body and dead skin on the victim's neck, and begins to wonder…

Sugar learns that Langston has left the club to her, and now Morgan tries to induce her to sell. Sugar humors the crime lord while continuing her plan of vengeance. In quick succession, she and her zombies dispatch two more of Morgan's men — by toss-ing one into a pen full of ravenous pigs, and by using a voodoo doll to force the other to stab himself to death. Sugar then anon-ymously sends the man's heart to Morgan in an urn.** Needless

* This intimation that the voodoo god has no use for Sugar's soul but instead wants her live body for his pleasure is a rather amusing (and exploitative) twist on the Voudoun practice of offering up one's body to be possessed (or "mounted") by the Loa so that the voodoo god can speak and act in the material world.

** This scene (along with several of the death sequences) was drastically cut for the TV version (renamed *The Zombies of Sugar Hill*) so that the viewer never sees what's inside the canister. According to Quarry, "There was a heart that was ripped out and it was pul-sating, bleeding, and steaming. It was a cow's heart or something that they'd cut out and put in. But it was all wired to sort of pulsate in the bowl." Unfortunately, this truncated version is the only one currently available since *Sugar Hill* has not been officially released on video.

to say, Morgan has become both angry and frightened at these attacks by his unseen enemy, and sends the rest of his gang out to find who is responsible.

While Detective Valentine, suspecting the involvement of the supernatural in these bizarre deaths, seeks answers from an expert on voodoo, Sugar continues her vengeful rampage. She kills the three remaining henchmen (via a straight razor judiciously applied to a voodoo doll, a coffin full of snakes, and an attack by the zombies).

Baron Samedi warns Sugar that Valentine is getting too close and subsequently puts him out of the way with a carefully placed pin in a voodoo doll, causing the nosy detective to fall down the stairs and break his leg.

Sugar then culminates her vengeance by luring Morgan and his girlfriend, Celeste (Betty Anne Rees), to Sugar's family mansion. There, Morgan is confronted by the zombies — as well as the now-reanimated corpses of his own men. The terrified mobster flees by jumping through a window. He races off into the swamp, but Sugar and her zombies trap him once more. In trying to escape Morgan falls into a pool of quicksand and drowns.***

"Well, woman," concludes Baron Samedi, "you've destroyed them all — nicely, neatly, superbly." The Baron then hands Sugar his silver-tipped cane as a memento and takes the screaming Celeste into his arms (as "the price I asked for our bargain"). With a hearty laugh, the king of the dead disappears.

The genesis of *Sugar Hill* began in Haiti itself, for that is where screenwriter Tim Kelly acquired his interest and inspiration. Kelly, a prolific playwright (with over three hundred published plays to his credit) who for a time made some extra cash penning blaxploitation pictures (and one other horror film, *Cry of the Banshee*, which he remembers as "a painful experience"), had visited Haiti several times and "was absolutely fascinated by the island and wanted very much to do something in that genre" (as he related to this author). Feeling that "there was nothing [in films at that point] that was really hooked into the basic aspects of the voodoo religion," he wrote a script in 1972 called *Black Voodoo* "that was absolutely loaded with historical stuff that was completely accurate." Paul Maslansky, a producer who was looking to direct his first feature, took Kelly's script to AIP and received the green light — after a significant rewrite, of course, to make the concept fit the exploitable AIP mold. "At that time," recalled Kelly,

***"Of course I got a mouthful of that crap," remembered Quarry about filming his death scene. "Jesus, but I couldn't get it out of my ears, I couldn't get it out of my hair. God, I was hours trying to wash that shit out. That stuff was very unpleasant."

"AIP was really intent on making *revenge* movies." So Kelly took *Black Voodoo* and (for the modest sum of $12,500) turned his historically accurate voodoo script into "the perfect wedding of the black exploitation film with something that was meant to be a little more serious."

Originally intended to be filmed in New Orleans (which makes more sense given its subject matter), the location was changed to Houston when AIP encountered "some sort of trouble with the teamsters," remembered Kelly. For the four-week shoot, director Paul Maslansky filmed in actual locations (real houses, hospital, office, mansion, etc.) rather than on a soundstage. As a result, the surroundings are realistic and more convincing than most, from the dusty deserted mansion to the eerie swampland.

Also convincing — and genuinely creepy — are the film's zombies. "They did good makeups on the voodoo people, the zombies," opined star Robert Quarry. With their bulging, filmy eyes a milky white, their hair matted with leaves and spider webs, and their pasty gray skin highlighted so that one can almost *see* the bones beneath the dead flesh, they present a terrifying image of death revived. In one shuddery shot, two of them sit up simultaneously from their shallow graves, turn their heads slowly toward one another, and *smile* –a horrible, ghastly rictus grim. These are creatures of *evil.*

Director Paul Maslansky (making his directorial debut *and* swan song — he never directed another picture though he continued as a highly successful producer) and cinematographer Robert Jessup take care with their supernatural charges, filming them to chilling advantage. In the resurrection scene, for instance, close-ups of gray hands poking up through the dead leaves of the mossy forest floor progress into atmospheric low-angled shots of the horrible corpses rising stiffly from the earth while the swirling mist turns the midday light into a hazy twilight punctuated by flashes of preternatural lightning.

As a voodoo film, *Sugar Hill* possesses more integrity than most — thanks to scripter Tim Kelly's genuine fascination with the Haitian religion. The story begins, for instance, with a voodoo ceremony in which authentically dressed devotees dance and whirl, some clutching sacrificial chickens or sacred snakes. Suddenly, one of the participants starts screaming ecstatically, apparently possessed by a Loa (a voodoo god or spirit), and the others rush to gather around her writhing body.

While visually intriguing and well-staged, this authenticity-minded beginning also illustrates the film's '70s quaintness: instead of the expected rapid drumbeats, we hear the Motown rhythm of "Supernatural Voodoo Woman" playing on the soundtrack. Though this musical anomaly remains more than a little disconcerting, the sequence ends rather cleverly when the dancers suddenly collapse and we hear applause as the camera zooms in on a sign reading "Club Haiti." It was all just an outdoor nightclub act.

In amongst the "hip" talk, screenwriter Kelly sprinkles some thought-provoking and credible dialogue. When Mama Maitresse admonishes Sugar, "Child, you have always been a *dis*believer; why do you now believe?" Sugar answers, "Because I want *revenge!*" making an interesting comment on the power of faith.

Later, in a ceremonial exchange, Mama Maitresse asks "where does the sun rise?" and Sugar answers, "In the east, Mama." The old woman continues, "Where does the sun *set?*" to which Sugar ritualistically responds, "In Guinee, Mama." Guinee was the term used by the Haitian slaves to designate their distant homeland in Africa and remains a symbolic Eden to the Voudounist.

The picture's subject matter apparently spooked some of its participants. "Some of the people were quite uncomfortable with making the film, because they really were a little upset about the voodoo aspect," recalled Kelly. "I'm speaking of the local people they used in Houston" who felt "that maybe you shouldn't fool around with this stuff." Nervous bit players aside, no serious mishaps (voodoo-induced or otherwise) occurred during the four-week shoot.

Sadly, *Sugar Hill* remains a decidedly flawed film. Beyond its appalling wardrobe and dated dialogue, the picture's main weakness lies in its acting. Apart from Robert Quarry, most of the major players are either amateurishly flat (the actors playing Morgan's henchmen) or too strained for credibility (Zara Cully as Mama Maitresse and top-billed Marki Bey).

According to AIP publicity, "Ms. Bey researched her part among various voodoo cults in and around the L.A. environs, thereby acquiring the proper authoritative menace to make her role as a voodoo high priestess believable." If so, it didn't work. Though pretty enough to look at, she brings little depth or distinction to her role. Bey was less-than-thrilled with her starring assignment, and this may have tempered her performance. In fact, co-star Robert Quarry remembered to this author that, "She hated it, hated the whole thing," even though Bey was the highest paid member of the cast (Quarry was second.)

Quarry had nothing but nice things to say about Ms. Bey. "Oh, Marki, she was darling. I don't think she ever made another movie. [She made one more, *Hangup*, released later this same year.] Marki had just come from the Pearly Bailey all-black *Hello, Dolly!*, playing Irene, the second lead. And she was as pretty as could be and was as nice as could be. We shot for about a week, and when the dailies started coming in [AIP president] Sam Arkoff didn't think she looked black enough so they had an afro wig made for her and darkened her makeup. So half of the time she had sort of light red hair with a very pale skin which they covered over. Well, I'm not sure, but Sam Arkoff with his usual class probably said, 'She don't look like a nigger to me.' Mr. Class. So they insisted they put her in an afro wig. She was beautiful."

Quarry, however, was not so enamored of his other co-star, Don Pedro Colley (playing Baron Samedi), calling him "one of the most pretentious bastards. He had a better dressing room than I did. That was in his contract, that he had to have a van and the whole thing. He was so full of affected shit. He behaved like he was the star of the movie. I mean, in *his* mind he was the star of the movie. So it was always 'Makeup! Costume! Wardrobe!' Don thought he was a *big movie star.*"

Colley's performance certainly reflects this "star" attitude. Colley plays Baron Samedi in a broad, exuberant fashion — wide-eyed, big-voiced, and full of theatrical poses and dramatic gestures. Though a voodoo god incarnate is an admittedly unusual role which calls for an unusual portrayal, Colley makes him something of a caricature and so fails to convince. (This concept of a voodoo god appearing on earth strays far from the Voudoun canon, since the spirits manifest themselves through human beings — via temporary possession — rather than owning corporeal forms themselves.) Colley's cause isn't helped by the echo chamber reverberation that his voice receives on the soundtrack — an obvious and distracting technical artifice.

As Morgan, Robert Quarry provides the only naturalistic and convincing performance in the film. His surface urbanity hides a brutal ruthlessness that periodically peeks out under the mobster's thin façade via his subtle expressions and unsmiling eyes.

Initially, producer Elliot Schick and director Paul Maslansky felt that Quarry was *not* the right actor for the part of crime-syndicate head Mr. Morgan. In fact, they felt he was not even the right *color*. "I was forced to do the movie," recalled Quarry. "I had a pay or play contract. They were going to make an all-black movie, but that meant that they were going to have to pay me and not play me, and Sam [Akroff] wasn't going to do that. Elliot Schick and Paul Maslansky, who were doing this all-black exploitation horror film, were not thrilled to suddenly end up with me playing the head of the Black Mafia. It made about as much sense as me playing Bernadette of Lourdes. So I was just suddenly flown off to Houston to do this movie. I hadn't even read the script. When I got there I read it and I thought what the hell am I doing playing *this* part? I mean, this was a black man's role. And they had a black actor set for it, but Sam said no, we'll use Quarry. And then as it turned out, it was a very happy working relationship with Paul and Elliot, because I was doing good work — even though it was just all wrong for the movie."

Despite everyone's protestations (including Robert Quarry's), Sam Arkoff's money-conscious insistence paid fine dividends, for Quarry's fine performance is one of the film's prime assets. "I was kind of amazed [when I saw it recently]," concluded the actor, "I wasn't that embarrassed by it."

Quarry brought more than just *his* acting talent to the part, he brought his *dog's* too. For the scene in which Morgan and his girl-friend receive the heart in a jar, the poodle Morgan plays with on the couch is actually Quarry's own beloved dog, Virginia. ("I had just done the play *Who's Afraid of Virginia Woolf?*, so when I got her I called her Virginia Woof.") Virginia was an instant success. "During rehearsal," remembered Quarry, "they opened the jar and she just kind of sat there. When they went for the take, I opened the lid and she went 'aaah' and jumped off the couch and ran [laughs]. She got a big hand, you know, everybody thought that was terrific she'd done that. She was a little ham." Virginia's "ham" paid off nicely for the canine thespian, for the director rewarded her sterling performance with a big steak at lunch that day.

Though he had small roles in a number of films, and scored some stage success in New York prestige productions like *Richard II*, *The Taming of the Shrew*, and *Who's Afraid of Virginia Woolf?*, Quarry didn't become a commodity until the low-budget drive-in horror *Count Yorga, Vampire* (1970) did unexpected blockbuster business. After the huge success of *Yorga*, AIP (who picked up the independent film for distribution) put Quarry under a five-year contract. The actor subsequently starred in two more vampire films, the inevitable *Return of Count Yorga* (1971) and *The Deathmaster* (1972), as well as *Dr. Phibes Rises Again*, *Sugar Hill (1974)*, and *Madhouse (1974)*. Quarry believes that AIP president Sam Arkoff saw him as a rival/successor to Vincent Price. This apparently caused some initial friction (which was soon smoothed over) between the two actors when they first worked together on *Dr. Phibes Rises Again*. In the late seventies, Quarry's acting career went on hiatus, due primarily to a serious car accident that kept him from seeking work for three years (as well as ending the life of his beloved poodle). The actor made a comeback of sorts when he began appearing in low-budget independents in the late 1980s such as *Cyclone* (1987), *Beverly Hills Vamp* (1989), and *Haunting Fear* (1990), usually directed by the prolific Fred Olen Ray (who affectionately refers to Quarry simply as "Uncle Bob").

Being one of the few whites in the predominantly black cast of *Sugar Hill* caused some problems for Robert Quarry (both on and off the set), even in the civil rights-conscious year of 1971. Just how far attitudes had *not* come was brought home to him one evening when he took his co-star to dinner.

"Marki [Bey] would never go out," remembered Quarry. "And I finally got her to go out to dinner with me one night. And she said, 'Well, I don't want problems.' We walked into a restaurant, a very fashionable restaurant. And we walked in at six o'clock, because Marki wanted to eat early and go to bed. So we went in there and there wasn't a person in the room and they said, 'Do you have a reservation?' And she was now in her light skin and red hair. Only in the South would anybody have known that she was 'a black,' an Afro-American. I said 'We'd just like to have dinner.' And I could see her shrinking back — because she knew what it was. He wasn't going to seat us because, you know, black and white do not *go together* in Houston, Texas, even in 1972 or whenever the hell it was. I mean civil liberties were in and they no longer had segregated toilets and segregated theater seats or segregated anything, but they had their own *way* of segregating themselves. So I said, 'Excuse me a minute Marki, I want to talk to this man.' And I went and I said, 'Listen, what is this *shit* that you're giving me? Is it because the young lady with me is black?' And he said, 'Oh no, no, no' and I said, 'I'll tell you what's up. I know a *lot* of people. You start screwing around with me with this ship and I promise you I'm calling every newspaper man and newspaper woman I know in this town and telling them what you've done.' 'Oh, we've got a table for you.' Well, now by that time the evening was ruined for poor Marki. She never went out again, she stayed in the Holiday Inn and ate breakfast, lunch and dinner there. It was just awful."

Though Quarry had spent several years in Houston with a respected theater troupe, he suddenly found himself *persona non grata.* "I was there making an all-black movie. And I had a lot of friends, very rich, very influential friends that I had made when I was there in 1960 [with the Alley Theater], ten years before. And they read 'Alley Theater actor returns to star in movie' — and it was called an 'All-Black Cast.' Well, I think they were so afraid I was going to bring a *nigger* to lunch. I mean, that was their attitude. Nobody called me, nobody asked me, nobody said, 'How are you?' They just *ignored* my being there since I was there under those circumstances. And it was just shabby."

Quarry ran into some racially oriented difficulties *on* the set as well. "Many of those people [who played the zombies and such] were local people they picked up there in Houston; they didn't use actors. So of course the black actors there hated me because I was calling them 'nigger.' I mean, that was what the script did. Well, it's all right for a black to call a black nigger, but they were seeing a *white* guy doing this. And they didn't know from acting. They thought that was what I was like, that it was *my* doing. So we had a very nice actor named Charlie Robinson [who played 'Fabulous,' Morgan's right-hand man], who was then at the Alley Theater and who later was in the TV series *Night Court* and *Love and War*. Charlie was the one who had to straighten 'em all out. So he went to all these extras — I mean, I thought they were going to *kill* me, they started *at* me — after I'd been screaming, 'back [off] you black bastards, you fuckin' coons,' or whatever the wonderful dialogue was, which as I said was perfectly all right to say if you were black but not for Mr. White Chops over here to be doing it. And he explained to them that it was just acting and that that was the part and what it was all about. So we settled down and it was all right."

"*Sugar Hill* was not a title I wanted," complained screenwriter Tim Kelly. "Sugar Hill was at one time the most wealthy area of Harlem, sort of the Beverly Hills of Harlem, and I thought that that title was kind of vague. I wanted something up there that said what it was all about — like *Black Voodoo*." Why AIP, a company famous for coming up with an exploitable title first and the movie second, would choose such a nondescript and unilluminating name as *Sugar Hill* for their new horror feature remains a mystery. (Had AIP co-founder Jim Nicholson still been on board, this film would have undoubtedly sported a much more effective — and exploitable — moniker, since Nicholson was renowned in the industry for his ability to create catchy film titles.) One possible explanation is that AIP was trying to follow in the lucrative footsteps of their previous vengeful-female blaxploitation feature, *Coffy* (1973). (If "Coffy" was good then "Sugar" must be better?)

Even so, the company seemed to recognize their marketing error, for their publicity refers to the film "proving to all and sundry that Sugar Hill is a curvaceous female creature — and not the geographical location the term so connotes…" At least when AIP sold the film to television, they changed the title to *The Zombies of Sugar Hill* (still no great shakes, but at least it gives the viewer a clue as to content).

AIP urged their exhibitors to promote *Sugar Hill* with such diverse tactics as a "Reptile Lobby Display" ("Obtain several snakes and place on display in your outer lobby with information pertaining to the picture and/or voodoo ritual"), a "Candy Bally" ("Print labels reading, 'I'm Sugar Hill, Try Me!' and affix to small plastic bags of any kind of candy"), and an "Ouanga or Voodoo Charm" giveaway consisting of "small plastic bones in a bag."

Plastic trinkets aside, the film itself didn't disappoint its intended audience (though modern viewers don't fare so well). Thanks to some well-staged and atmospheric sequences, Robert Quarry's convincingly ruthless portrayal, and the genuinely frightening zombies, Sugar Hill still remains a fairly entertaining blast-from–the-past curiosity.

Roland remembered that "of those scripts reaching the silver screen, *Sugar Hill* was fun to write. We had to become voodoo experts and deal with the mafia at the same time. I should say, we knew little about the subject of the mafia and did a lot of reading up on it — the zombies and voodoo stuff, we even took a trip to Haiti, which was an eye opener. Our original working title was "Black Zombies Meet the Mafia." Also, it probably lasted longer — still going — and brought in more $$$. *The Brothers O'Toole* was pure fun because it was pure western.

"But writing a movie script is pure drudgery. It usually goes thus:
"1) submission and acceptance of an idea
"2) contract, under Screenwriter's Guild rules
"3) submission of story (8 to 20 pages) outlining the whole thing
"4) 1st script
"5) 1st rewrite
"6) 2nd rewrite
"7) 3rd rewrite
"8) final script
"9) additional dialogue
"10) director's cuts
"11) credits
"12) budget
"13) SHOOT!

"Every step of the way is a bloodbath and often becomes silly. Also the system is a terrible time waster. Can you imagine the writer's state of mind at the 3rd rewrite conference? And very often the writer has to change the scene from upstate New York to sub-Sahara 'because we still have a lease on some sand dunes east of Mexicali!!'

"His produced and never-produced works came mainly out of his head. The ideas for the three black-oriented movies came mainly from his producers."

Chapter Eight

It was because of the heartbreaking process of film collaboration and Tim's true love for living art that kept him penning the plays as fast as his typewriter ribbon could scroll. His biggest hits included an adaptation of *M*A*S*H*, the ear-catching title *Help, I'm Trapped in a High School!*, and the very popular *The Butler Did It*, which found productions around the world. *Butler* was a spoof (with no butler) much along the same plot and character lines as Neil Simon's *Murder by Death*: a group of famed sleuths, not quite with the same names as the famous ones — Miss Marple in Tim's version becomes Miss Maple, etc. — are invited by one of their own to a murder mystery weekend, when things go terribly wrong ... It was such a hot commodity that Tim wrote a sequel, *The Butler Did It, Again*, and the inevitable musical, *The Butler Did it Singing!*

Tim's own description for the sequel, published by Baker's Plays, shows just how in tune he was with his audience. He was also obviously a good advertiser of his own wares.

"Written by the 'master of the outrageous comedy mysteries,' this is a much requested follow-up to the ever-popular 'THE BUTLER DID IT.' Publisher and socialite, the indomitable Miss Maple rents a plantation house, complete with menacing alligator, in the frightening swamplands of Louisiana. She wants to introduce her latest literary discovery, Ruth Dice, who has written a first novel entitled *Conversation with a Ghoul*. Ruth has only contempt for the guests. [They include] classic detective prototypes like tough Chandler Marlowe, chic Manhattan couple Rick and Laura Carlyle, [and] westerner Tony Tallchief. Ruth dismisses Louie Fan ('Telephone like corpse. Both dead.') and gentle Father White ('Tea and biscuits, anyone?') as has-been hacks. Naturally, she's the perfect candidate for murder. However, it's the bizarre owner of the house of secrets, Jasper Van Dine, who's discovered in the parlor with a scalpel (once belonging to Jack the Ripper) in his back! WHODUNNIT!? It's up to the flaky detective writers to unravel the puzzle. Chills, thrills, alibis, clues, motives, and dazzling plot twists fly about the stage like pies-in-the-face. Nothing is what it seems to be and you'll need a scorecard to keep track of who's who and what's what. Smoke and mirrors, fun and games — from start to finish. Bring a seat belt!

'A crazy gumbo of off-the-wall dialogue and nutbrain action. Very funny Stuff.' — Theatre Laurel Prompter"

Tim wasn't the only writer in the family. Roland kept a diary of their time together, called "The Breakfast Book" (usually written over coffee in the morning). The journal provides a rather detailed, but often sketchy, account of the couple's daily life.

Roland states, "Mostly it was a reference: 'When did I see that guy at Warner Bros.?' 'Where were we when Ed Lester called?' Also, it was a diary of my personal activities — I did a lot of counseling activities at the Hollywood Gay Community Services Center, and at the Hollywood Gay Church, Metropolitan Community Church's Crisis Intervention Center."

The following is an excerpt from May of 1970:

"5-26. Tim up late. Still bad weather. I took Volks to shop for oil grease, straighten bumper. Fooled around Holly Blvd. Home at 2. Tim began, finished rough of 'The Rat & the Raven.' Also talked to Harry, Jack Stewart. We went to Regeancy at 6. Tacos at 10 and home.

"5-27. Wed. Up at 7:30. Tim at 9 and off to Schwab's offices at Paramount: 'Lawrence Gordon Productions.' I cleaned house, did large laundry. We are awaiting word from Fla. about Patty. She is to be operated on for 'a lump' in the breast. Mail just brought: package for Tim from his mother, sample ballots, lots of campaign but nothing else. Tim called at 3, home at 5. Larry G. called at 5:30. The day went well. 'Born Tough' now back in Arizona – possibly 'OLD TUCSON' 8:30 TO SEE 'You & Whose Army.' Many old Arizona friends. Sally, looking old, old. Tim spoke briefly to Quillen — will put up costumes if his group does 'Song of the Dove.' We ate late — after midnight at Stein & Surloin. Just terrible meal. Home and to bed at 1.

"5-28. Thurs. Up at 7:30, Tim up and calling Larry Gordon at 8:30 and off at 9:30. Mos. Pinkie Jackson from Housekeepers Helpers is here, cleaning. The mail brought contract from French on 'The Silk Shirt,' the first check ($1,000 gross) from Larry, and loads of voting stuff. Larry Gordon called at 2:30 for Tim. Pinkie left — the best cleaner we ever had — at 3:45 and Tim in at 4:30 to nap. Couldn't get Larry. I walked the dogs and at 7:30 Tim left to interview some x-motorcyclist club president. He got in about 11. The interview was a waste of his time. To bed about midnight.

"5-29. Fri. Up at 7. The sun was shining, but clouds came up. 'You & Whose Army?' got a bad review in The LA Times. Tim up and called Larry at 8:30. He was checking to make sure we had plenty of copies of Step outline for 'Cry Tough.' To Schwab's at 9, with Pal in the back seat. Home and to work on 'Born Tough.' In the PM we went over to N. Hollywood to see 'Merton of the Movies' done by the Penny Gaffers Dramatic Society at the North Hollywood Playhouse. Got spaghetti after at our favorite place in Sherman Oaks. Met nice guy Toby Anderson, the president. Home about 1 AM.

> *"5-30. Sat. Up to pleasant warm day. Tim up at 8:30 and off to Schwab's. Home and finished work on 'Born Tough.' I proofed and tightened and we went over it again. The Step outline finished finally. We had hamburger dinner and to bed early.*

> *"5-31. Sun. Up late. Tim and Pal delivered Step outline to Bob, had coffee at the Coffee Cup. Jay Schaffer called. In the PM Tim cleaned house and we went to see 'The Landlord' at 8. Dinner at Barney's Beanery and home about midnight.*

> *"6-1. Mon. Up late to beautiful day. Tim off at 10 and I'm beginning to get things together for Phoenix trip Wednesday. It is hot and we didn't do much — sunbathed and I picked up the house. Mail brought TV [Guide] and checks and little else.*

> *"6-2. Tues. Election day and we discovered our phone out."*

One close neighbor was director Edward Dmytryk (*The Caine Mutiny, Raintree County*, etc.). Roland states, "I can't say Dmytyrk and Tim were close friends — they were too much alike, but they were friends and saw quite a bit of each other, especially during the years we were neighbors. Eddie wrote several textbooks on movie production and I believe he asked Tim for his opinion on them. They met at our homes and walking the mountain each day."

Tim took Dmytryk's Doberman, Co-Co, when the great director died, and later wrote the play, *Always Poodle*, to help himself get over Co-Co's passing.

"Tim was so devastated he couldn't talk about her for months," Roland states. "I think it was published, but I'm not sure Tim even tried to get it published. Incidentally, the September before he died, Tim got another lady Dobie and named her Co-Co. Spookily, Co-Co II died suddenly two weeks after Tim's death!"

Tim kept in touch with various celebrities through his work. He knew the cast of *The High Chaparral* (Cameron Mitchell, Leif Erickson, Henry Darrow). Another friendship that came out of that television writing job was Max Wesley Harding.

"My first meeting with Tim Kelly was in 1969 when he was story editor for *The High Chaparral* TV series," Max recalls. "As a budding actor, I thought I might increase my changes for an acting job if I wrote a show for the series. In pitching my storyline, the first thing I noticed about Tim was that he seemed like just an everyday kind of guy. Certainly not what you'd expect from some TV big wig. Even more surprising was the fact that he actually presented my story to the producers, only to be finally vetoed.

"I continued to drop by the studio to see Tim every time I had the idea for a 'hot story.' On each visit Tim gave me not only encouragement but sound advice on how to go about writing a sellable story. Our friendship grew and before long I was allowed to call him at home with all my questions and ideas.

Unfortunately for Tim, I chose him to be my proofreader and editor for nearly everything I wrote for the next twenty-six years.

"Tim had a magical way of simplifying all my creative problems. The most important thing he ever told me when I apologized for my bad spelling was, 'Your job is to tell an interesting story. We have lots of people who can spell.'

"Tim's basic and creative approach to solving problems within the field of creative writing allowed me to become a published author over a dozen times.

Edward Dmytryk and Co-Co.

To this very day I still find myself wanting to call him on any writing problem I run into. I also still have every letter he wrote to me as a reminder of my early struggles and [to remind me of] just who pushed me past my simple little problems and self doubt."

But as Roland states, "Tim did not consider himself a celebrity. He *enjoyed* his anonymity and was always careful to respect it in others. Living in Hollywood, we were constantly cutting trails of film people and he *never* ever pushed into their space.

"A couple of times he was requested to sign a program or something. He was pleased, but also embarrassed, and he was naturally a courteous man. His ego? Separate it into two parts: 1) of his work he was boundlessly egotistical. He came with the secure knowledge that his plays were superbly crafted and that he was an outstanding craftsman; 2) of himself he was insecure. Boston-Irish, middle-class, low income. I've seen him agonize over what to wear. He honed his social graces and sometimes had trouble with small-talk situations. He really didn't like dealing with movie people, but with theatre people he could fascinate an individual, a group or an auditorium full — for hours!"

Tim was also friendly with Harry Hickox (character actor in *The Music Man*), Vaughn Taylor (*Psycho*, TV's *Mr. and Mrs. North*), Al Hammer (movie extra who doubled for Groucho Marx), and Mae West. For the latter, he wrote a treatment, reprinted in the Appendix because of its double rarity (unpublished, and definitely not for kids), in 1979 called "She Couldn't Say No." As Tim explained to this author, "You may find 'She Couldn't Say No' amusing. It's a film story for Mae West (are you too young to remember her?). During the making of *Sextette* (sigh) everyone in town said La West was making a comeback — naturally the comeback was not to be but I concocted this epic for her nonetheless."

He finally gave up film writing, since, as Roland states, "His heart was always in his plays! And after a time, that's what paid the rent. His screenwriting just tapered off gradually, but his plays were a steady flow."

Tim firmly believed that theatre people were not film people, the latter always going for the big bucks, bringing in more writers for rewrites, etc., etc. He told one reporter, "The most successful theatre in L.A. would be a drive-through theatre where people sit in their cars."

Chapter
Nine

On May 23, 1977 Tim received a positive and almost typical letter from one of his many publishers. This time, Performance Publishing Company wrote:

> *Dear Tim,*
>   *Everybody liked your play AMERICAN GOTHIC and we would be happy to publish it under the terms of our regular royalty contract. We have a big surprise for you — we have no changes to recommend and believe it requires only routine editing. The climax has real impact. I hate to ask, but on either this or THE CONVERTIBLE TEACHER we would like to use a pseudonym other than Bibolet.*

Playwrighting was paying off. He didn't need the hassles of Hollywood. As Roland states, "For all his varied 'irons in the fire,' Tim never ceased being essentially a writer of plays. And I don't really recall any need to rework his stuff. Especially after he got so much stuff published, his publishers pretty much accepted what he sent. His way was to get a rough draft through his typewriter, then go over it line by line. The script would look like a hospital case with the clipping, scotch tapes and blue pencils, but that is the way it would go to the typist.

"He worked mostly at high speed. I have a notation in my journal — '8-17-70: Tim began *Second Best Bed*. 8-18-70: Finished *Second Best Bed*.' That's pretty typical."

The *complete* process could be lengthy, however. "It takes me about six to eight weeks to get a play down on paper," Tim told *Drama-Logue*, "but I've been thinking about it for years. I like to get in the right frame of mind. For example, if I'm writing a western play, I surround myself with western objects. I play western records. Being a playwright is like being a religious fanatic — you just keep going."

When Tim used the setting of Nogales, Arizona, for *Everything's Jim Dandy*, the April 18, 1978 edition of the *Evening Daily Nogales Herald* proclaimed on its front page: NOGALES HAS ITS OWN HOLLYWOOD PLAY! It gave a bio of Tim, citing him as the grandson of Charles Ringling (a former executive of The Ringling Brothers' Barnum and Bailey Circus), plus a brief resume of the play's previous rave reviews. *Point West Magazine* had this to say: "Kelly probably knows the Southwest as well as any writer today... his people are genuine... his ear for their conversation right on target. Whether he's dealing with the rodeo or life in border communities, he translates his subject into vivid memory."

But for the most part, critics were not kind to Tim's work, often refusing to separate high art from the business of theatre: giving audiences and teachers what they wanted was (and perhaps is) too popular a concept to those expecting every play to be a Tom Stoppard thinker or a Neil Simon one-liner riot.

"Tim was hurt by critics," says Roland. "He felt he was pushed around by them in Phoenix and in L.A."

Tim told *Drama-Logue* in 1982, "The playwright has to get in the frame of mind where the most important thing is to appeal to the audience, not the critics."

He practiced what he preached.

He was disenchanted that the theatre was thought of as an elitist place. With civic theatres supported by tax money, most people could not afford to buy a ticket; and that applied not just to theatre, but to dance and music, as well. If these things were totally subsidized, he thought, not only could everyone see them, but kids would come out of school with a greater appreciation of theatre, dance and music.

In the early-'80s Tim was a part of the Los Angeles Actors' Theatre playwrights' unit, working on plays-in-progress, staging works-in-progress to fine tune his new wares, plus to give something back to the kids who were making him a regional, and national, success.

In 1981 Tim incorporated Tim Kelly, Ltd. in the state of California, but dissolved it in November of 1993.

Roland stated, "In my opinion Tim didn't change very much. His lifestyle stayed pretty even, whether he was Tim the Beginning Writer or Tim the Hitmaker. He always was working his ass off, always planning, always thinking of his work. He always was a bit nervous, a bit insecure. He had always strong faith that he would achieve fame before he died. I heard him say this many, many times."

For all his fame, Tim remained basically a shy man, although he did socialize.

Glenn Schmoll recalled, "As a masseur in a San Francisco chiropractic office, I was very blessed to meet and massage headliners from both Las Vegas and Broadway. These people, I was already aware, were famous. I was fortunate enough to meet Tim Kelly on a social basis so he didn't need to be wary I was pursuing his friendship for what I could get from such an association.

"At a fund raiser I attended, I saw this man who definitely stood out in the crowd. He wore a pair of tight, worn Levis with several tears in them. I remember when I saw his hair it reminded me of a shiny piece of coal and he exuded masculinity like few men I've known. Yet, when he approached me, he was soft-spoken with a slight Boston accent with a very self-confident attitude. He was the kind of man that left a lasting impression on both men and women, and I wouldn't have been surprised to have seen him mount his horse and ride off onto Sunset — since this was a Hollywood function.

"I was privileged to be a guest in his home several times before I moved to San Francisco. I remember the house had a super masculine feel about it and with the Navajo rugs and western trappings; I could have easily been in a typical Arizona ranch home. Some twenty-five years have passed since I was there, but I know there was at least one western saddle prominently displayed in the living room and another at the entrance as well as other 'horsey' paraphernalia.

"Like many of the people I've met who are involved with the entertainment world, Tim was extremely modest, but proud of his accomplishments. When he knew I was a 'dabbling writer' and was truly interested in him and his work, he was happy to share suggestions and then produced a few of the scripts for some of the movie posters I'd seen on the walls in his den and bedroom.

"The last time I saw Tim I was honored to be his guest at the Theatre Exchange in North Hollywood for a performance of *Everything's Jim Dandy*, described in the program as 'a look at Life and Love in the Rodeo Ring.' I had been raised in the country of Colorado where rodeo was taken for granted as entertain-

The house of Kelly.

ment. At the time I never thought of how much it was cruelty to animals. The theatre itself had once been an auction barn so the venue was quite appropriate to the theme of the story. It was Tim's only play I've ever seen and sitting next to the author added to my enjoyment of the young cowboy's awkward approach toward maturity.

"Tim and I exchanged both Christmas cards and phone calls after my move to San Francisco. I tried several times to get him to come visit, but was never successful. His schedule and mine just never meshed on my few visits to Los Angeles.

"Some of us like Gurdjieff are blessed to meet 'a few remarkable men' and Tim Kelly was in that category for me. The longer I live, the more I cherish how bonds are formed — and even more wonder at how strong they remain over time and distance. Tim Kelly occupies a special place in my memory and thoughts and I'll be forever grateful he entered my universe."

Roland agreed that "Tim wasn't *at all* hype-oriented, but he had to deal with people who were. I can't even recall him going after media attention. It made him nervous. But he did feel that Los Angeles never gave him credit where it was due. For example, I remember once he had three plays going at the same time in the L.A. area and there was only one (negative) mention of it."

But —

Teachers loved him. Jim Phillips, director of drama at Annunciation Orthodox School in Houston, Texas, explained, "I had planned to do *A Midsummer Night's Dream* with my eighth grade acting students. The class size exceeded its limit by nine women. I had to divide the class into two units and find a play for that exact number. In searching the catalogues, I came upon *Ladies of the Tower*. The time period was perfect to present alongside Shakespeare's comedy: a drama of the Elizabethan court, and a comedy of Elizabethan theater on the same bill. The girls liked the characters in it, the teachers liked the historical relevance, and as a director, I liked the simplicity of the production values. The play was a success."

Ladies of the Tower.

Several students from the *Ladies of the Tower* production gave their thoughts on the play:

Elizabeth Easterly: "My role was that of Queen Catherine Howard. I had a lot of fun making the production, although getting the British accent down was more difficult than I anticipated. I thought the play was very profound and tragic, maybe too much so for actors our age. The maids added a nice touch of comedy, and the bare stage effect worked well."

Courtney Jay: "I really enjoyed performing this play because it brings back real historical stories. Horrible things happened to these women and this play really helps to tell their stories on a more personal level."

Stephanie Putnam: "Tim Kelly wrote a play that worked very well. The one thing I would change about the play is to have each character do something instead of just sit in a chair while each person talks."

That lack of "action" was the only negative comment from cast members.

Tim claimed that one of the reasons he liked writing for youth so much was that it got them acting and reacting and away from "watching that goddamn" television, which he likened to a narcotic: Not only is television too passive as a spectator art form, all of the glitz is one-dimensional. On stage, with a large cast, many voices and a colorful backdrop, there is a magic happening that *cannot* be replicated on a flat screen.

At age 55, Tim addressed the Playwrights Forum's ninth annual Playwrights' Conference in Catholic University's Hartke Theatre. Its focus was his specialty: "Making a Living by Writing for the Stage." He warned that writing in this arena would remove the "art" quality in people's eyes. He likened it to buying clothes from the Penny's catalogue rather than at Neiman Marcus.

"One is not superior; they're just different," he said.

Tim further explained his own anti-elitist viewpoint: "Basically, I want to embrace my audiences. I want them to feel secure with me. I design my mysteries especially for people who are not too sophisticated — a plot they can follow, interesting characters — no 'smartsy' stuff. With all my plays, I try to avoid anything that's terribly topical, so that they can be performed twenty-five years from now. You're not going to find profanity or vulgarity…or anything salacious. And I sure as heck stay away from religious topics."

He wrote juicy parts for actors to show off for five minutes, and generally steered clear of elaborate sets and costumes and time periods requiring such. But he was strictly against writing to appeal to everyone: "That's like wishing for more blue-eyed blond Chinese. I treat each play like a marriageable daughter. Some marry Prince Charming, some end up walking the streets, but I do the best I can to get them out into the world."

Florine Atwood, who directed Tim's *Ladies of the Tower,* was one of many school directors who found that Tim the writer "did a good job giving directions on how to enter the stage. Someone who has never directed a play before could follow his directions easily. I followed most of his instructions. When you look at the pictures you will see how I set the stage. If I was not doing it for competition, I would have only used the stools like he suggested. I ended the play by having the characters circle the chopping block and leaving like they were leaving the tower forever. It is a very good play. The teachers at school enjoyed it because it taught the history of [Queen Anne Boleyn, Queen Catherine Howard, and the Queen Mother Elizabeth] that had been confined in the Tower of London.

"I liked how the play was written. It was a short play, but it said a lot. None of the dialogue was wasted. I performed this play for the elementary, junior high and high school. All of the students were interested and could tell that the ladies and queens were ghosts. I am picky about the plays I choose. I had read several and was going to choose another play, but I was drawn back to this one each time."

The March 23, 1989 response Tim Kelly received from Eldridge Publishing Company's Nancy S. Vorhis (editor) was typical of correspondence from his school play publishers: "Several weeks ago I saw a local production of *Don't Rock the Boat* and I was bemoaning the fact Eldridge hadn't heard from you in some time. So it was a great delight to receive your letter and an even greater treat to read *It's a Howl.*

"We love it — the flexible cast, the humor, the snappy dialogue, and all the stage action. So many full-length submissions just lack that special sparkle which yours have. *It's a Howl* looks like a real blast to perform! And the complete notes for the director are a sales plus, too."

It was this breadth of product that kept — and keeps — Tim Kelly plays in play.

Chapter
Ten

Even with all the school performances (and the royalties rolling in), Tim kept entering play contests. On July 11, 1990, he was informed that his *Crimes at the Old Brewery* had been chosen for a staged reading by the Festival of Firsts Playwriting Competition. It was staged at the Sunset Center on September 16th in Carmel-by-the-Sea, California. Encouraged by its success, he then entered *Crimes* in the Elmira College Third Playwriting Award competition and won its first prize of a production and $1,000. All expenses were paid by Elmira College for Tim to travel to Elmira, New York for a performance. His play had been chosen from 306 entries from across the United States, as well as Canada and Sweden, and premiered to a sold-out crowd during the college's Founder's Day weekend over March 7-10, 1991. While at Elmira, Tim gave several talks on playwriting and was guest lecturer in at least one directing class. And as the guest of honor at a black-tie dinner, he was presented with a Steuben Glass dragon, which represents imagination.

The First Lady of the American Theatre, Helen Hayes (who received her first honorary degree from Elmira College) attended the gala, and wrote to Tim afterwards:

> *This morning I at last caught up with you through Ken Beers. I was very frustrated not to see you after the play to tell you how much I enjoyed it. Alas, it can never be a New York production because of that great line of actors bowing at the end and the salaries they would represent. It is fun and I hope it will be enjoyed through many university players and community theatres.*
>
> *For a long time I have been putting my trust and hopes into Community theatres to keep the theatre alive all over our land. The Broadway theatre is so impoverished that we cannot afford anything more than casts of two to three. Therefore, I am most grateful for a chance through Elmira College to see* Crimes at the Old Brewery.
>
> *Helen Hayes*

The mystery-thriller plot took place in Lower Manhattan's Five Points District, in a squalid tenement that was once The Old Brewery, but which is now (in the play, of course) housing murderers, robbers, lunatics, beggars, prostitutes, pickpockets, dope addicts, drunks, ragpickers and homeless children.

Tim had a true affinity for mysteries. In a way, they were his specialty. He gave his thoughts on the genre — and, briefly in turn, on his understanding of formula — in his "One On The Aisle" column from November 20, 1959.

> Ever since the [1866] debut of the mystery-melodrama, *The Black Crook*, combined with a theatreless girlie show to produce America's first musical comedy called *The Black Crook Extravaganza*, the mystery play has been in and out of favor. The genre really hit its stride in the post-World War I era and made the

financial scene in the 1920's. Most of these plays, e.g.: *The Bat, The Cat and the Canary, The Thirteenth Chair, The Gorilla,* and *Spider's Island,* are still with us. The relics are offered in revival simply because new "thrillers" are not being written.

The "thriller" plot is basic. A group of people are held in one given location, usually a big house cut off from the mainland by a rising storm, a native uprising, or mysteriously locked doors. One by one [the characters] are eliminated and the audience is asked to guess why and by whom. [The phrase] "The butler did it" owes its popularity to the popularity of these works (1912-1937). World War II, which shattered so many illusions, put the screws to the "thriller." The mystery-melodrama was not for mature or sophisticated audiences, so the plays switched to the "psychological thriller" formula, where the audience is aware of the murderer and must watch his or her psychological downfall, e.g.: *Duet for Two Hands, The Shop at Sly Corner, Gently Does It, Crime Without Passion,* and the slickest of the slick, *Rope.*

One of the last pure "thrillers" produced on the New York stage was Agatha Christie's *Ten Little Indians,* and by that time [1943] even Christie has switched to the psychological viewpoint of the "thriller," encasing it in a smart setting, e.g.: *Witness for the Prosecution.*

Personally, I have always enjoyed the old school where some unknown person nicknamed "The Avenger," "The Serpent," "The Mad Monk," or "The Eye" was creeping around in the attic looking for the lost Ethiopian jewels.

To save face, mystery writers for the stage now gag it up and play it with a light touch. I protest! Bring back "The Avenger" and the terrified dinner guests, who arrive to find their mysterious host hanging from the 12th century beam in the tower room.

The Mousetrap at the Phoenix Little Theatre until tomorrow evening is a combination of the old "thriller" and the new psychological mode with heavy dashes of humor. It's London's longest-running show. I feel Miss Christie is working at the assembly belt, however. Adapted from her short story, "Three Blind Mice," *Mousetrap,* like *The Hollow* (another Christie chestnut), is routine. Nevertheless, "thriller" devotees owe the Little Theatre a note of thanks for presenting this "Who-Done-It."

But it would be fun to see the old school of "thriller" again.

We could have this island, see, and during a terrifying storm a Coast Guard boat could crash on the rocks of Lighthouse Island, long since deserted. Three men stagger into the abandoned lighthouse. A table has been set for three. Candles flicker. "Hello!" they shout. A bat flies; a pane of glass crashes. Then, slowly, down the winding stairs comes an aged crone carrying a 19th century

kerosene lamp. "Be seated, gentlemen," she says, "we've been expecting you." Music is heard … a door opens …
> Won't sell?
> I know, but it would be fun.

For Tim, writings mysteries *was* fun, and profitable.

"Financially, we were careful," says Roland. "We bought the Lookout Moun-

Tim relaxing at the Nogales, Arizona home, circa 1975.

tain house in 1965 and had it paid for by 1975. His plays started bringing in the big *dinero* about 1995, and he invested in CDs mostly, and mutual funds and saving accounts. Death taxes got the bulk of this money.

"He didn't frame his first royalty check. We needed the cash to pay the rent. He had sort of a W.C. Fields-type of secrecy about his money, talking to no one, scattering his accounts around, and worrying about finding himself in Walla Walla, Washington without funds."

But even with financial worries over, Tim was not quick to adapt to the new technology available to his means. "We were at a party around 1975," says Roland. "The host had a computer and he sat Tim down at it and began to teach him and show him how much a computer could help a writer. Tim's eyes glazed over and he acted like the infernal machine might affect his sanity. He later told me he could not, *would not* change his system and he didn't, to the end.

"In 1990 I asked him if I could give him a word processor for Christmas and he forbade such a thing. He did not have a fax. His VCR activity was limited to switching the TV to VCR, inserting the tape, and rewinding and ejecting the tape."

Chapter
Eleven

"Tim was a sick man for his last three or four years (1994-1998)," states Roland. "It was Trigeminal Neuralgia. He said it was like an ice pick being struck into his left jaw. He was under medication — pain killers — which seemed to do nothing but give him more pain, and made him nervous, worrisome, sleepy and miserable. He looked so puffy and like he was just about to burst into tears all the time. A simple 'How are you today?' would result in an outburst. Boy, it didn't affect his output, did it? He kept talking about cutting back and never did. He died writing plays!"

Tim mentioned to Steven Fendrich of Pioneer Drama that he wanted to slow down. But as Roland admits, "Tim always intended to take care of himself and was always embarking on a health program, but it never worked. The demands upon him and the waiting around [were] so destructive that our lifestyle was very bad. Hours were impossible, we both drank too much — until we finally both went on the wagon. Since our house was on a very steep hillside, just walking the dogs each day was a very good workout for both of us. We ate out a great deal, so we had lots of food that wasn't too healthful. And then toward the end, Tim's health was overshadowed by his terrible illness. He was heavy his last year of life. I think it was fluid retention. The medication was for pain, not curative. This memory saddens me."

His last years brought a few comforts, though. On April 23, 1995 Tim joined playwrights Jerome Lawrence, Robert E. Lee and others being inducted into the College of Fellows of the American Theatre, recognizing "eminent individuals whose life work constitutes a truly outstanding contribution to the profession." Every year since 1965 a small group of individuals have been recognized at an annual meeting at the John F. Kennedy Center for the Performing Arts in Washington D.C.

Michael Sutton was a friend of Tim's for almost 20 years and was the only witness to the events leading up to his very unexpected and untimely death.

"On December 7, 1998 I walked into Tim's study at one-thirty in the afternoon to ask him a question. I had a tendency to come in two or three times a day, though sometimes I wouldn't see him for two or three days. He was making out Christmas cards at the time. I came in to ask him a question and all of a sudden he just pushed himself up from the desk to respond to me. He almost stumbled, then he fell and he seemed as though he was trying to catch himself on the way down, but he didn't, he just fell over on his left side. He went into convulsions, almost as if he was having a seizure. I could tell he was having a problem breathing. Immediately, I grabbed his nose and gave him six deep breaths of mine, blowing into his mouth. That didn't seem to help much. I immediately called 911 and they came in about eight minutes. He was 'jerking' — a slight gasping for breath.

"I went down the driveway, figuring they might have a little problem finding the number. It was the Fire Department. They didn't drive up, so I called to them and they ran up the driveway, about 300 feet. I brought them in and they straightened him out on his back and tried to insert something into his throat so he could breathe. His office was very crowded so there wasn't enough room to work in, so they dragged him out the east door onto the east patio. They tried again out there, but from where I was standing I could tell they had it, perhaps, in the wrong part of his throat because his stomach began to swell as if the air was getting into his stomach rather than his lungs. I hollered at them right away and they pulled it back out and tried it again.

"By that time the paramedics came; I don't know if they called them or if my 911 called both. They did a few things on him and decided they'd better get him to the hospital. But I believe at that time, when they put him in the ambulance, he was already dead.

"He had mentioned a couple times a nervous condition he had in his face which became very painful: Trigeminal Neuralgia. He said the pain was so severe that when it happened at times when he was out with company, he would just have to excuse himself and get away and bear the pain. He never mentioned how long it would last. I saw him take quite a few different medications and at least *some* vitamins. He'd have them all laid out there on the kitchen counter. When the Fire Department arrived, they wanted to know what medication he was taking, so I grabbed all the bottles and showed them."

Tim's request in his December 1994 will was that he be cremated, with no viewing, funeral or memorial service to follow. Shortly after Tim's death (on December 7, 1998), Roland Bibolet, as his Executor, began to attempt to compile the Tim Kelly writings. This was a monumental task. Tim was not a keeper of records — he was not a file clerk. In the succeeding years, this effort has resulted in an impressive library. At their Santa Cruz County home a 125-year-old adobe storage shed has been converted into a repository of Kelly manuscripts and letters.

"We have his desk and typewriter and we have at least one copy of all his known printed plays," says Roland. "But there are occasional surprises. Last year, we had an inquiry regarding a Kelly play titled *Dog Eat Dog*. I haven't located it yet. Some works have two or three titles, some manuscripts have no title. It is tough."

The TJK library is a pleasant room filled with movie posters, theatre announcements, and mementos near and dear to Tim.

"It is my memory room," says Roland.

Tim in his office. PHOTO COURTESY OF BILL FRANCOEUR.

Chapter
Twelve

Death killed the body, not the talent. The plays of Tim Kelly are still going strong. And they show no sign of slowing.

Just from Pioneer Drama's report of the time period of May 1, 2003 to April 30, 2004, there were 900 performances of Tim's plays. Roland states that "a great deal of Tim's success was fueled by the phenomenal growth and success of Pioneer. And Tim's product pleased them. They printed just about everything he sent them. Of course, Sam French and others used his stuff, too. But I guess the bottom line is Tim's plays are good. Here it is, almost ten years after Tim's death and his work is still being performed, still popular."

Tim is recalled not only for his body of work, but for the courtesy and professionalism he showed his colleagues, neighbors and fans. Consider the following testimonials…

Arthur L. Zapel
Editor-in-Chief for Meriwether Publishing Ltd.
Contemporary Drama Service

Many years ago Tim Kelly phoned me to ask why we had never published any of his plays. He told me that almost every play publisher had published one or more of his works. "Why hadn't we?" I checked our records and discovered that Tim had only submitted full-length plays to us. At that time our emphasis was almost completely on one-act plays. I got back to him and told him we'd give a second look to his full-length plays and any one-acts he had available. He sent both. We liked both and published them. That began a friendship of about fifteen years. We published a play each year. He was a "pro" in every sense of the word. We'd discuss ideas by phone and he'd write the play; we would publish it.

Tim never went half way. He never expected special consideration based on our long tenure together. Each play he sent included a cover design lifted from other copyrighted art publications. It made the submission look complete. We, of course, had to redesign the covers with original art; Tim never complained.

Tim's plays were consistent sellers — usually parodies of well-known works. Tim did it so well. He amplified a story theme, adding laughs along the way, and never infringed on the original work. He had an eye and an ear for what would work well on stage. I don't know if he was ever an actor himself, but I do know he knew what was "playable." He always included ideas for staging, costumes, and special effects.

We met face to face only once — at a convention. We talked at length and became phone pals thereafter.

It's been difficult for us to replace Tim's steady work, but his influence still prevails. Our other playwrights often try to learn the craft from his works.

Patricia Stacey
Tim's neighbor and widow of Big Band musician Jess Stacey

Tim and I met about forty years ago [around 1962] as members of Lookout Mountain Associates, a group of property owners living in our small Hollywood Hills canyon. LMA was a wonderful neighborhood organization. We had meetings with speakers from Fire and Police departments, arranged a CPR course conducted by the Red Cross, had plant sales to raise money, as well as a purely social annual Oktoberfest.

Jess and Pat Stacey at Tim's Lookout Mt. home. October 1971.

Out of the larger civic LMA membership evolved a smaller group of ten or twelve of us who became very close friends. Together we celebrated all birthdays, anniversaries, Halloween, Christmas, Fourth of July, etc. It would take only a few phone calls to assemble a lively group for spur-of-the-moment cocktails.

Tim arranged a festive theater party for us to attend one of his plays being performed nearby, with supper afterwards. Great fun! Many of Tim's plays were presented many miles away out in the San Fernando Valley. Tim did not have a great sense of direction but said it was easy for him to find this theatre — he just drove to the end of the freeway and then he was there. Sometime later Tim told me he'd gotten lost going to the theatre because the freeway had been extended and when he drove to the end he had no idea where he was.

Tim had a keen interest and curiosity about local events. If the power went out, Tim investigated and could report that a fallen tree down the street was the cause. Or if there was a fire, Tim could give the exact location while radio and TV furnished incorrect information. So, if we wanted to know what was going on, we called Tim.

Tim and I were the youngest in our group, so as the years rolled by our friends began to die. And then there was only Tim, Bernard Scott, and I — but the three of us still celebrated Christmas together. In the years before his death, Tim and I talked on the phone two or three times a week.

About a week after my husband died in 1995 I was in a strip mall having photocopies made and ran into Tim. He asked if I had time to stop for coffee. We settled down with our coffee and Tim said, "Pat, do you need any money?"

I thanked him and said I didn't, but I will never forget his kindness in offering such tangible help.

I loved Tim and so deeply regret that the last few years of his life were spent in pain and suffering. When he died my first thought was that now there was an end to all that pain — my second thought was I have lost a dear friend forever.

Every year on December 7th I mourn Tim, but more importantly, I remember the fun and happy times we shared.

Steve Fendrich
Owner, Pioneer Drama Service

Some of my favorite memories as publisher of Pioneer Drama Service were my chats with Tim. Some were mapping out his plays for the year. I knew that Tim could write anything. Thus, we would decide on a full-length show, melodrama, Christmas play, one-act play, and so on. We would also decide on a musical where he would write the book and, most often, we would pair him up with composer Bill Francoeur. I would often call him up and request a show based on a title or subject matter. For example, when I wanted a one-act concerning gun control, I would have the script on my desk in a matter of weeks.

The main thing, though, was that Tim was my mentor. After my father (Shubert) passed away, Tim would be a support system. We would have discussions over the phone, many over two hours long, where we would discuss Pioneer's potential. As Pioneer began to grow, I knew that I could count on him to help fill voids in our catalog. For example, when I wanted an audience participation murder mystery, I received the one-act *Three Doors to Death* in a number of weeks.

When people began to ask if Tim actually owned the company (he had so many plays with us), it was decided that we would start using pseudonyms. Many people have done shows by Robert Swift, Douglas Winters and Vera Morris. I once asked Tim where he came up with the names, especially Vera Morris. Vera was a poor woman in Spain that he met. Every year Tim sent the woman some money. One of my favorite memories of the playwright Vera Morris was when we received a call from someone who had done a Vera Morris play. "I'm so glad that you have a sensitive woman writing these shows," she said.

How did Pioneer and Tim find each other? In the mid-sixties, my father started a playwriting contest to attract new writers. Tim's play *Not Far from the Giaconda Tree* won the award. From there, the relationship began.

I only saw Tim a few times in my life. One year, when my wife and I visited Tim at his home in Hollywood, he showed us around. One of his prized possessions was a picture of him and Helen Hayes. Tim had won the Elmira College National Playwriting Award for his show *Crimes at the Old Brewery*. The award was presented to him by Helen Hayes. After Tim passed away, I was asked if I wanted anything to remember him by. I now have the picture of him and Helen Hayes in my office.

Tim died on December 7, 1998, exactly ten years after my father. Two days after he died, his Christmas card came to us. However, he had been working on a 1920s script to be adapted into a musical. The show was entitled *Flapper*. No one could find the script. We knew it had been written. Finally, two weeks later, the script was found. It had been given to a typist who was not

aware that Tim had died. When she came to his house with the script, she was not aware of his death and, as I was told, cried. The script was sent to our office and Bill Francoeur put his heart into making the show one of his best. To this day, *Flapper* is still one of our biggest sellers.

I once asked Tim what play of ours was his favorite. I was surprised at his answer. It was *Puss in Boots*.

Tim was an extraordinary writer. Though our relationship was mainly over the phone, I'll never forget his constant support. His flexibility as a writer was astonishing. He not only wrote *Krazy Kamp*, he also wrote adaptations of *Sleeping Beauty* and *Cinderella*. His

The last picture of Vera Morris. She predeceased Tim by a couple of months.

melodramas will forever remain popular. Schools and community theatres are still putting on performances of *Alias Smedley Pewtree* and *The Ballad of Gopher Gap*. His one-act plays such as *Laffin' School* is still a favorite. Overall, we have close to 150 shows with his name on the cover. Tim Kelly may not be with us [in body], but he will forever be with us in spirit as hundreds of his plays will be done for years to come. In one of our phone calls, we pondered whether a Tim Kelly play was being done every day of the year. I wouldn't be surprised if that were true.

Ben Ohmart
Owner, BearManor Media

I include myself in this grouping because I had a brief but pleasant exchange with Tim Kelly in 1997 — just one year before his death. As an aspiring playwright, I was eager to learn from a man who had made a bankable name for himself in a decidedly challenging profession. I submitted a series of questions, which he answered and returned. This meant even more to me later when I discovered just how ill he had been at the time. As I reread these questions with a more mature perspective, I can see just how green a fan I was. But my respect for my subject was genuine.

Here is that interview in its entirety.

> *Query:* Is there anything you've always *wanted* to write, but haven't tried yet?
>
> *Kelly:* No.
>
> *Query:* Have you ever collaborated on a play (musicals where you write the book, but someone else does the music doesn't count)?
>
> *Kelly:* I've collaborated on a couple of plays. Didn't like it. Doubt if I'll ever do it again.
>
> *Query:* Have you written any plays for radio? If not, why not?
>
> Kelly: No. It's a specialized and too-limited market. Most plays we hear on radio are from other areas.
>
> *Query:* Do you have any hobbies not associated with writing?
>
> *Kelly:* Not really — with the exception of ranching, which I don't consider a hobby.
>
> *Query:* Do you use a computer? What kind?
>
> *Kelly:* I am computer illiterate. I work via pad and pencil and IBM Wheelwriter 3.
>
> *Query:* Any rituals (like only writing with one pen or having to eat six hard-boiled eggs) that you do before writing?
>
> *Kelly:* No rituals, unless stalling as long as possible can be considered a ritual.
>
> *Query:* Do you walk, run, bike or chew on the furniture for exercise?
>
> *Kelly:* Walk/swim.

Query: Do you listen to music while writing?

Kelly: Rarely, if ever.

Query: Finish this lyric: "If I had a hammer, I'd ..."

Kelly: Put it in the garage.

Query: Favorite band/singer/music?

Kelly: None.

Query: Do you mow the yard or do any yard work yourself? Relaxing or time away from your writing?

Kelly: Minimal yard work.

Query: How much fan mail do you get per week or day?

Kelly: Varies. Roughly 12/15 letters per week.

Query: Would you say you have *something* in performance year round, or are there slumps?

Kelly: Production rate is consistent.

Query: What exactly did you give to the University of Wyoming for their Tim Kelly Collection?

Kelly: They maintain a file of everything I send them. In time, they will receive letters, etc.

Query: Any pet charities?

Kelly: Doberman Rescue and a few others I contribute to, but it varies from year to year.

Query: Do you get to NYC often?

Kelly: No. I used to visit New York 2x each year, but not lately. I don't like to travel.

Query: Do you have a particular favorite play you've written, or are all your children equal?

Kelly: My favorite play is the one I'm working on at the moment.

Query: Are you a coffee, liquor, or soft drink guy?

Kelly: I try to stay away from caffeine. Once in a while [I'll have] a glass of *Vino Blanco*.

Query: Have you tried (m)any of the little presses as markets for your plays?

Kelly: No.

Query: When Pioneer or Art Craft or etc. do t-shirts or posters of your plays, do you get free copies?

Kelly: If I request them. One can only have so many t-shirts — then it becomes pointless.

Query: Have you been listed in *The Guinness Book of World Records* for your prolificacy? If not, why not?

Kelly: *The Guinness Book of World Records* doesn't consider the number of plays I have published to be significant. So, I have not been listed.

Query: Do you know if the losers get anything out of entering play contests?

Kelly: Certainly, experience, if nothing more. After all, someone is actually reading their material — and "considering" it.

Query: When was the last time you were approached to write for TV or film, and what did they want you to do?

Kelly: About two months ago. A thriller set on the Great Barrier Reef. I passed. I no longer do any TV. The thriller was a film project.

Query: Are you at that point in your career when you can get a play published without a performance? Or do you not want to do that?

Kelly: I never publish a play that hasn't been tested in performance.

Query: Do you seek out schools near to you for world premieres of plays you've just written?

Kelly: Sometimes. However, I have a list of schools (assuming it's a school play) across the country who are more than willing to premiere a Kelly play.

Query: That's all for now. Thank you, Tim!

Kelly: You're welcome, Ben.

Roland and Tim in Egypt, 1977.

After Tim died, I contacted his life partner, Roland Bibolet, at his home in Nogales, Arizona. I explained that I wanted to compile a book on Tim's life and career. Roland was only too happy to comply. He supplied me with the many rare photographs included in this volume, and was wonderfully candid with me at all times. The following is the transcript of a conversation I had with him about the love of his life.

Query: What was the usual arrangement between Tim and his publishers?

Bibolet: The estate has a separate contract with the publishi companies for *each* published play; historically, each company arranges the copyright and guards their rights.

Query: Do you recall any specific plays or projects he had a particularly hard time on, for one reason or another?

Bibolet: One of his early ones (Tim always considered it a major opus) was *A Darker Flower*. It was performed, but isn't in print. He was in labor with it until after it closed in New York City — [that was in] 1957, I think. He was writing on it and sleeping with it before he was out of school. Other challenges included:

Everything's Jim Dandy. It is a good play and was performed and had good runs in the LA area but he kept tinkering with it to make it better. He had movie hopes for it.

His plays about Richard Francis Burton. One of his titles is *A Secret Garden*. It was popular on the college circuit. He read extensively about Burton and read much of Burton's stuff just to get ready to write. Another title is *Raggedy Dick & Puss*.

Late Blooming Flowers (Checkov spinoff) had a good run in Hollywood, but Tim was always tinkering with it.

Welcome to the Casa, about a ranching family in South Arizona. It had a good run in Hollywood. I believe it was finally printed, but he kept working on it and working on it. I think I was more involved in *Casa* than anything else he wrote.

Query: What kind of TV shows and movies did Tim like to watch? Did he have any favorites?

Bibolet: He enjoyed Harrison Ford movies. I think he could be a boy again watching one. He went to a lot of movies and always theatre, theatre, theatre. He didn't hesitate to walk out, though, if he felt so moved.

He often said "when I'm at the movies or watching TV, I'm at my desk." He would usually critique what he had been watching to me. He read every "trade" daily so he was well-informed about TV and movies. We belonged to the Writers Guild West Movie "club" and went to the Guild almost every Sunday evening to see a not-yet-released movie. Typically, he would wind up writing at 4:30-5 p.m. and watch news and cartoons until dinner and then TV (with some work) 'til eleven or midnight. I think he enjoyed old reruns the most.

Query: Did he have a favorite play or author he admired?

Bibolet: When I first met Tim, Eugene O'Neill was peerless, but after we sat through a couple of his (for me) endless dramas, I think he changed his mind. Tennessee Williams was a favorite — *One Arm* especially. And *Suddenly Last Summer*. He probably was envious, too, about Williams' commercial success. He enjoyed reading Dotson Rader's *Cry of the Heart*, but just couldn't understand how Tennessee got so hooked on drugs.

[Tim] was a Shakespearean, too! He did two or three plays with a Shakespearean base (*Second Best Bed* and *Ladies of the Corridor* come to mind). And Chekhov he admired.

Query: Did he have any hobbies, other than writing?

Bibolet: He always had two or three books going (biography, theatre, movies). We used to go to the beach a lot until his skin problems developed. He would have ridden horses more, but it just wasn't handy enough. He tried to walk a bit every day. Good eating, good conversation. He was active in the Lookout Mountain Associates (we both were) and formed some lasting friendships in our neighborhood.

Query: How about favorite actors/actresses?

Bibolet: The dowager in the Marx Brothers movies [Margaret Dumont] and the old gal who played Miss Marple [Margaret Rutherford] and the witch in *The Wizard of Oz* [Margaret Hamilton] were favorites of his. I don't know if he ever met any of them. Generally, and very privately, I think Tim didn't like

Roland Bibolet, August 31, 2005. "This is a view of the old ranch adobe barn I've converted into a TJK repository. Everything you see here was pretty much as he had it in Hollywood. Now I'm trying to organize everything into a library. Note I'm using a cane now. I turned eighty-six on this date."

actresses or actors. It takes a *lot* of ego to be an actor and a special personality. Someone who must be center stage, all lights on me all the time. He loved Elisabeth Bergner's voice, Ethel Merman's brass, Helen Hayes' stage presence, Edna Mae Oliver's method acting skills. He could write more easily for actresses than actors. In my opinion, his feminine roles were closer to Tim than his male roles. He loved those old Laurel and Hardy tapes you sent him — "fat and skinny," he called them. Slapstick always amused him.

Query: What kept Tim tied to Arizona so much? Something more than the weather?

Bibolet: Tim lived in Phoenix, AZ from July '56 'til we went to Spain in June '59. He taught school, worked for the Salt River project, wrote for the *Arizona Republic, Arizona Highways, Phoenix Point West* and acted and directed in various little theatre groups. He returned to Arizona about 1960-61 and lived there

(Phoenix again) until he won the scholarship at Yale in '65. We then moved to Hollywood ('66?) where he remained, returning for visits to Nogales and Phoenix on occasion. His sister Patsy had moved to Phoenix from Orlando. The attraction? Some of it he got from me. My Arizona roots are deep. Much of it he developed as he wrote. He adopted the ways and words of the West. He loved the freedom, the air and the scenery. He hated the heat,

Roland Bibolet, Patsy Kelly Schultz and Beverly Griffith in Phoenix, circa 1975.

so he had a problem. And importantly, Arizona and its history gave him much material for his plays and books.

Query: Did Tim go to church? Did he have a philosophy about "greater" things?

Bibolet: Tim was raised a Catholic, but when I met him he declared himself an agnostic. He did believe in some "greater thing." He did believe he and I would "meet again." This he expressed many times to me. He contributed to an organization dedicated to separation of church and state. He went to church only with me when I was so involved with the LA gay church. (I'm an atheist, but I did counseling at the Metropolitan Community Church there.)

Query: Do you have any favorite plays that Tim wrote?

Bibolet: Favorite? No. I think his wisdom, ability as a writer, humanity, humor, beauty and fascination are spread throughout all his works.

Query: You were involved with theatre a bit, weren't you? Did you ever try your hand at writing plays? Or would two writers in the house have been evil?

Roland today.

Bibolet: The first and last play I wrote was in the eighth grade. I played in high school plays, community theatre in Nogales (*The Night of January 16th, The Ghost Train*) and Phoenix (*Death of a Salesman*). One writer in the casa was chaotic — two would have been nuclear.

Query: How was division of household chores (garbage, shopping, fixing things around the house, etc.) divvied up?

Bibolet: The household revolved around Tim's writing. Result: I did most of the day-to-day chores. We ate out a lot and had a pretty busy social schedule. Also something called "Port-a-maid" delivered a maid to our doorstep. She moved the dust around, got into whatever was in the bar, unloaded her problems (in English and Spanish) and charged mucho *dinero*. We had a washer/drier so laundry was no problem. I did the gardening. Since our home is on a hillside, there is no lawn. We have avocado, pine acacia, oak and all the greenery of the coast. Fixing things? Sorry, neither of us was adept at the nail and hammer. I kept a list of S.O.S. people for clogged drains and leaky roofs.

Query: Do you believe Tim was proud of his accomplishments?

Bibolet: He was always proud of his success. He must have had a good formula. His plays are still as popular as ever. I wonder how many Americans actually earn a living by writing plays."

Appendix A
The Many Credits of Tim Kelly

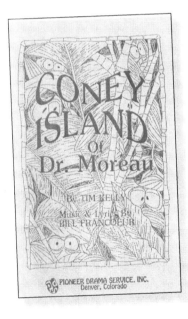

Plays
(all full-length unless noted)

The $1.35 Avocado *(1-act)*

The 3 1/3 Musketeers

18 Nervous Gumshoes

A-Haunting We Will Go

Abracadabra, Aladdin! *(musical)*

The Adventure of the Clouded Crystal

The Adventure of the Speckled Band

The Adventures of Rikki-Tikki-Tavi

Airline

Aladdin and His Wonderful Lamp *(musical)*

Alas! Alack! Zorro's Back! *(musical)*

Alias Smedley Pewtree, or The Villain of Glitter Gulch

Alice's Adventures in Wonderland

Aliens Are Coming! Aliens Are Coming!

Always Marry a Bachelor

The Amazing Adventures of Dan Daredevil

Amy Goes Army *(1-act)*

And Here She Is Tapping Her Way into Your Heart *(1-act)*

Archie of the Amazon *(1-act)*

Attack of the Killer Grasshoppers *(musical)*

Attack of the Giant Grasshoppers *(1-act)*

Ballad of Gopher Gap

Bang! Bang! You're Dead *(1-act)*

A Barker Flower

Barrel of Monkeys

Barry Dunn

Be Beautiful — But Dumb

Be My Ghost

Beast of the Baskervilles *(1-act)*

Beau Johnny

Beauty and the Beast

Bedside Manor *(musical)*

Belle and Blue Duck

Belle of Bisbee

Billy Jack

Bloody Jack

Blue Suede Paws *(musical)*

Bluebeard Had a Wife

Bride of Frankenstein

The Bride of Frankenstein Goes Malibu

The Brothers O'Toole

Buckshot and Blossoms

The Burning Man

The Butler Did It

The Butler Did It, Again!

The Butler Did It, Singing *(musical)*

The Butterfly

Calling the Hawk

The Canterville Ghost

Captain Fantastic

Captain Nemo and His Magical, Marvelous Submarine Machine

Case of the Curious Moonstone

The Cave

Charleston! *(musical)*

Charley's Charmers

Charming Sally

Chickenman

Cinderella Meets the Wolfman!

Cinderella's Glass Slipper *(musical)*

Clipper (original title: The Rum Lot)

The Clods of Hopper

The Comedian

Coney Island of Dr. Moreau *(musical)*

A Connecticut Yankee in King Arthur's Court

Connecticut Yankee — The Musical *(musical)*

Courtesy of Contemporary Drama Service

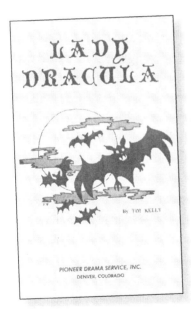

The Convertible Teacher (written as Keith Jackson)

Country Gothic

The Crazy, Mixed-Up Island of Dr. Moreau

Creeps by Night

The Creepy Creeps of Pilgrim Road (*musical*)

Cry of the Banshee

Curse of the Werewolf

Curse You, Otis Crummy

Dark Deeds at Swan's Place, or Never Trust a Tattooed Sailor

A Darker Flower (*aka* The Lily)

The Day Christmas Disappeared from Evergreen Town

The Deceitful Marriage

Destiny

Dirty Work in High Places

Dirty Work on the Trail

Ditch Day

Dog Eat Dog

Don't Be Afraid of the Dark

Don't Rock the Boat (*straight & musical versions*)

Don't Say No to the U.S.O.! (*musical*)

Dr. Jekyll...Please Don't Hyde! (*musical*)

Dracula

Dust of Eden (*aka* Welcome to the Casa)

Egad, the Woman in White, or Sealed in a Madhouse

The Empty Chair (*1-act*)

The Enchanted Sleeping Beauty (*musical*)

The Enchantment of Beauty and the Beast (*musical*)

Enter Pharaoh Nussbaum

The Eskimos Have Landed

Everything's Groovy! (*musical*)

Everything's Jim Dandy

The Face on the Barroom Floor

The Fall of the House of Usher

First on the Rope

The First Wife

Flapper! *(musical)*

The Floor Is Bright with Toys

Fog on the Mountain

Follow That Rabbit *(musical)*

Frankenstein

Frankenstein Slept Here *(1-act)*

The Frankensteins Are Back in Town

Funny Bones!

A Fussin' an' A-Feudin' *(musical)*

Ghostchasers

The Gift and the Giving

A Gift from Mars *(1-act)*

The Glass Slipper

Going…Going…Gone with the Breeze! *(musical)*

Gone with the Breeze *(musical)*

The Great All-American Disaster Musical *(musical)*

The Great Ghost Chase *(musical)*

The Green Archer

Groovy! *(musical)*

Guess What I Did Last Summer *(musical)*

Hansel and Gretel

Happily Never After *(1-act)*

Hawkshaw the Detective

Hee Haw Hayride *(musical)*

Hello from Mongo

Help! I'm Trapped in a High School!

Here Come the Cows

Hi, Ho, Robin Hood *(musical)*

Hide and Shriek

High School Dropouts from Outer Space *(1-act)*

The High School that Dripped Gooseflesh *(musical)*

Courtesy of Contemporary Drama Service

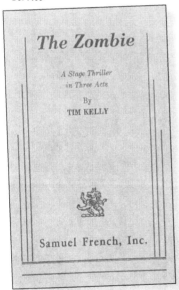

Courtesy of Samuel French, Inc.

Hollywood Hotel

Horray for Hollywood

Horror High

Hospital

The Hound of the Baskervilles

How Santa Got His Christmas Tree

How to Get Rid of a House Mother

The Hunchback of Notre Dame

The Hunchback of Notre Dame Goes West (1-act)

Hurricane Smith

Hurricane Smith - The Musical (musical)

I Know Where the Body's Buried

I Want My Mummy! (musical)

If Sherlock Holmes Were a Woman

If These Walls Could Talk

Incident at Taormina

The Incredible Bulk

The Incredible Bulk at Bikini Beach

Inspector Incognito and the Kansas City Kid (musical)

The Internal Teen Machine (musical)

The Invisible Man (1-act)

Is There a Doctor in the House?

The Island Way

It Was a Dark and Stormy Night

It's a Bird … It's a Plane … It's Chickenman (1-act)

It's Bigfoot (1-act)

Jack and the Giant (musical)

Jack and the Magic Beans

Jingle Bells Jury

The Jungle Book (2 versions)

The Jungle Book (musical)

The Keeping Place

Kilroy Was Here (musical)

King Midas and the Palace of Gold (musical)

King Midas and the Touch of Gold
King of the Golden River
Kodiak Flapjack
Kokonut High
Kokonut Island *(musical)*
Kokonut Kapers *(musical)*
Krazy Kamp
Krazy Kamp - The Musical *(musical)*
Ladies of the Tower
Lady Dracula
Laffin' Room Only
Laffin' School *(1-act)*
Laffin' School Reunion *(1-act)*
Lagooned
The Lalapalooza Bird
Lantern in the Wind
Last Chance High *(musical)*
The Last of Sherlock Holmes
Late Blooming Flowers
The Legend of Pocahontas
The Legend of Sleepy Hollow
Lemonade Joe Rides Again
Les Miserables
Life on the Bowery
The Little Luncheonette of Terror *(musical)*
Little Miss Christie *(musical)*
The Little Princess
The Little Princess — The Musical *(musical)*
Live a Little *(musical)*
Lizzie Borden of Fall River
Locomotion, Motion, Doctor Gorilla & Me
Look Who's Laffin'
Lost in Space and the Mortgage Due, or Revenge on the Launching Pad
Love Is Murder
Lucky Dollar, Private Eye
Lucky Dollar — The Musical *(musical)*

Lucky Lucky Hudson and the Twelfth Street Gang (*straight & musical versions*)

Lumberjacks and Wedding Belles (*musical*)

The Mad Adventures of Mr. Toad (*musical*)

The Madman's Goya (*1-act*)

The Magical Land of Oz (*musical*)

Mark Twain in the Garden of Eden (*1-act*)

A Marriage Proposal — Western Style (*1-act*)

The Marvelous Playbill

M*A*S*H (*also as a 1-act*)

Masha

The Masked Canary (*musical*)

Meet the Creeps

Memorial (*1-act*)

Merry Murders at Mountmarie

Money, Power, Murder, Lust, Revenge, and Marvelous Clothes (*musical*)

A Monster Ate My Homework

A Monster Ate My Homework - The Musical (*musical*)

Monster Soup, or That Thing in My Neck is a Tooth (*1-act*)

Mountain Fever

The Mouse and the Raven

Mr. Toad's Mad Adventures

Mrs. Wiggs of the Cabbage Patch

Murder at the Goon Show

Murder at the Masquers

Murder by Natural Causes

Murder Game

Murder in the Magnolias

Murder on Ice

My Gypsy Robe

My Name Is Rumpelstiltskin

My Son Is Crazy — But Promising

The Mystery of the Black Abbot

Nashville Jamboree *(musical)*

The Natives Are Restless

Navajo House

Never Trust a City Slicker

Nicholas Nickleby

Nicholas Nickleby, Schoolmaster

The Nifty Fifties *(musical)*

Night of the Living Beauty Pageant

No Opera at the Op'ry House Tonight, or
Too Good to be True

Not Far from the Giaconda Tree *(1-act)*

Oliver Twisted

The Omelet Murder Case *(musical)*

The Overcoat

Oz! *(musical)*

The Paper Bag Bandit Rides Again

Pecos Bill and Slue Foot Sue

Peril at Pumpernickel Pass

The Phantom of the Op'ry *(straight &
musical versions)*

The Picture That Was Turned to the Wall

Pictures from the Walls of Pompeii

The Pied Piper of Hamlin

Pocahontas

The Prop Trunk *(1-act)*

Puss in Boots

Raggedy Dick and Puss

Rascals Under the Big Top

The Ratcatcher's Daughter, or Death
Valley Daze

Recess! *(musical)*

The Remarkable Susan

Renfield of the Flies and Spiders

Reunion on Gallows Hill *(1-act)*

Robin Hood

Robin Hood, the Musical *(musical)*

Rock Around the Block *(musical)*

Rocky of the Rainforest *(musical)*

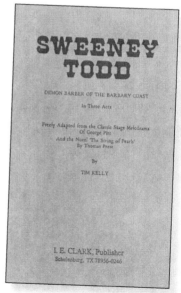

Courtesy of I. E. Clark Publications

Courtesy of I. E. Clark Publications

Rogue of the Railway
Rumpelstiltskin Is My Name *(musical)*
Santa and the Wicked Wazoo
Santa's Big Trouble
Say Uncle, Uncle Silas
Second Best Bed
The Secret Garden *(musical)*
Secret of Skull Island
The Secret Sharer *(1-act)*
Seven Brides for Dracula *(musical)*
The Seven Wives of Dracula *(1-act)*
Shake with a Zombie *(musical)*
Shakespeare Comes to Calamity Creek *(musical)*
The Shame of Tombstone
Sherlock Holmes
Sherlock Holmes and the Giant Rat of Sumatra
Sherlock Meets the Phantom
Silent Snow, Secret Snow
The Silk Shirt
Slambo
Sleepy Hollow *(musical)*
Small Wonder
Snake in the Grass
Snow White and the Seven Dwarfs *(straight & musical versions)*
The Soapy Murder Case
Son of the Mounties
Song of the Dove
The Spell of Sleeping Beauty
Spider for the Fly
Spring Break
Squad Room
Squad Room Blues *(musical)*
Stop That Villain!
Stop the Presses… or She's Not My Type
The Story of Hansel and Gretel *(musical)*

Street Story *(1-act)*
Summer's in the Air *(musical)*
Sundown Alley
Sunset and Laurel *(1-act)*
Sunset Trail *(musical)*
Sweeny Todd
The Tale That Wagged the Dog
Tap Dancing in Molasses
Teenage Night of Living Horror
Teens in Tinseltown *(musical)*
Terror by Gaslight
That's the Spirit
This Old House *(musical)*
Those Wedding Bells Shall Not Ring Out
Three Doors to Death *(1-act)*
Thumbelina
Tied to the Tracks *(musical)*
Time and Time Again *(musical)*
The Time Machine
The Timid Dragon
Tiny Thumbelina *(musical)*
Toby Tyler
Toga! Toga! Toga!
Tom Sawyer
Trapped in a Villain's Web
Treachery at Cartilage Creek
Trick or Treat
Trouble in Tumbleweed
The Trouble with Summer People
Two Fools Who Gained a Measure of
Wisdom
Tumbleweeds *(musical)*
Under Jekyll's Hyde
The Underground Venus
Unhappily Ever After *(musical)*
Unidentified Flying High School
The Uninvited
Up the Rent

Courtesy of Contemporary Drama Service

The Vampyre

Varney the Vampire

Victor Hugo — In Rehearsal

Victoria at 18

Videomania

The Villain Wore a Dirty Shirt

Virture Victorious

W.C. Fieldsworthy - Fooled Again

Wagon Wheels West *(musical)*

Wash Your Troubles Away *(musical)*

We Like It Here *(musical)*

Web of Women

Welcome to Bedside Manor *(musical)*

West of Pecos

Westward, Whoa! *(musical)*

What's New at the Zoo?

Whatever This Is - We're All in it Together

The Wild Colonial Boy

While Shakespeare Slept

Who Threw the Overalls in Mrs. Murphy's Chowder?

Who Walks in the Dark?

Who's Minding the Psychedelic Store? *(1-act)*

Widow's Walk

The Witch Who Wouldn't Hang

Wolf at the Door

The Woman in White

The Wonderful Wizard of Oz

Wrangler Ranch *(musical)*

XYZ Files *(1-act)*

Yankee Doodle

Yard Sale

You Ain't Nothing but a Werewolf *(musical)*

You Can't Stamp Out Love

Young Dracula … or The Singing Bat *(musical)*

Yours Truly, Jack Frost

The Zombie

Zorro's Back in Town

Screenplays

Bizarra — Strangest Creature That Ever Lived

The Blood Red Shamrock

Bogash

Born Tough

Bottom Line *(written as Lowell H. Jermstad)*

The Brothers O'Toole

Cry of the Banshee

Curse of the Voodoo

Dart

Everything's Jim Dandy

Get Fisk

Gooseflesh

The Hands of Dr. Maniacal

Hell on Four Wheels

The Mercenary

Sugar Hill

The Whitechapel Horrors

Story Ideas

After the Sign of the Ram

Bikini Bandits

Call Him Fury

Comes the Revolution *(written with Sid Kuller)*

Devil Dancer *(written with Bill Porter)*

Don't Scream, Edna, Don't Scream

Enter Pharaoh Link

The Great Balloon Race

The Suicide Club

Thanatos

What's Going On Out There?

TV Scripts

Hec Ramsey ("Hummy Sing")

Here Come the Brides ("The Last Winter")

The High Chaparral ("Bad Day for a Thirst"), 1967

The High Chaparral ("The Kill Agent"), 1968

The High Chaparral ("The Lion Sleeps"), 1968

The High Chaparral ("Ride the Savage Land"), 1967

Nakia ("The Sand Trap")

Powder Keg ("Rough Road from Galveston")

Awards

ABC-TV (grant)

Alumni Achievement Award, Emerson College

American Broadcasting Company Fellow, Yale University

Aspen Playwrights Conference Award

Bicentennial Playwriting Award, University of Utah

California Festival of Arts Drama Award

Colonial Players (Maryland) Best Play Award

Columbia Entertainment Company, Best New Play

Creative Writing Award, National Endowment of the Arts

David Nederlander Playwriting Award

Elmira College Best New Play Award

Emerson College Playwriting Alumni Award

Forest A. Roberts Playwriting Award, Northern Michigan University

International Thespian Society Award

Moorpark Theatre Best Play Award

National Endowment for the Arts (*grant*)

Nederlander Production Company Playwriting Award

New England Theatre Conference Award

Office of Advanced Drama Research (*grant*)

Pioneer Drama Service Playwriting Award

Playwright Grant, Office of Advanced Drama Research

Playwriting Award, Northern Kentucky University

Santa Fe Theatre Corporation Playwriting Award

Sarasota Centennial Drama Award

Sergel Drama Prize, University of Chicago

Texas Community Theatre Stage Center Award

Theatre Americana Best Play Award (*twice*)

Wayne State University Best Play Award

Weisbroad Playwriting Award, Alexandria Theatre

Appendix B
Selected Writings

Theatre Reviews

One On The Aisle
August 7, 1959

Censorship is the deadliest foe of theatre. And censorship and theatre have been at it for quite a number of years. What is it that piques censorship groups to barnacle on live theater, movies and books is something that is open to a variety of explanations, but these media seem to be the favored stamping grounds of censoring zealots. Censorship groups do not always object on "sex themes." Mores, political significance, religion, and regional attitudes are all in season. Thus, it is, that we find in so late a year as 1957 a Cape Cod theater tent's license being revoked because its production was Schnitzer's carousel love poem, "La Ronde" ("The Dance of Death"), written originally in the late 1890's. The stated objection: "Conducive to licentiousness."

In the twenties and thirties the guardians of public morals put the heat on New York mayors to tighten up. Thus, we saw a five-year period of citizens' groups deciding what show was morally fit for the theatergoer and what show was not. In some cases shows that had been running well over a year were found "objectionable" and closed. They even took Mae West off to the city jug for a few months. She had been appearing for over a year in an intriguing soap-opera-melodrama with the fetching title of "Sex." (Mae even donated a library to the jail.)

I don't know if the citizens' group censored the library or not, but there was probably some kind of to-do about the selections. The film, "Lady Chatterley's Lover," (about as erotic as a Dwight Fiske record) was recently judged "unfit" by a New York City Censor (paid, incidentally, by the city of New York). His judgment was overruled by the courts. Chicago would never see "Anatomy of a Murder" if the courts hadn't overruled a censor group that banned the film on the grounds of "offensive dialogue." And let us not forget that only last year the Phoenix newspapers reported that the city police were considering banning that hoary epic dealing with the effects of soil erosion, "Tobacco Road." Steinbeck supplied the squelch: "It's nice to know someone's still reading it."

The saddest aspect of the whole sorry business comes when a work that is slightly conventional is quietly avoided in deference to a censorship mentality and a "please everybody cupcake" shows up on the boards.

The result: No "Three Penny Opera," "Desire Under the Elms," "Suddenly Last Summer," and "I Am a Camera."

Only last week I heard someone say it would be nice to see "The Mikado" again.

One On The Aisle
September 11, 1959

Any guesses as to what's the longest running show in New York?

If you've guessed "My Fair Lady," you're wrong by over 800 performances. The show that has them standing in line, and has had for the last six years, is Kurt Weil's, Bertolt Brecht's "The Threepenny Opera," and there's not a current Broadway musical from "Gypsy" to "Redhead" that can top it. It makes everything else on the New York stage look like amateur night at the Elk's Lodge.

"The Threepenny Opera" was originally written in the eighteenth century by John Gay. The opus then was called simply, "The Beggar's Opera," an acrimonious musical commentary on the way of the world. The plot is simple enough: Captain MacHeath, a scoundrel and master criminal, falls for Polly Peachem, a fair-haired charmer. But Polly's parents, the Svengalis behind the "beggar business" in London, will hear none of it for fear it will ruin their "name." MacHeath, not to be deterred, marries and beds Polly, and the in-laws start on a campaign to blot him out. But then, as Brecht's text points out, "in this world of flesh, the police are naturally the consorts of Macky." And so MacHeath (a.k.a. "Captain MacHeath," "Macky," "Mack the Knife") escapes his traps and waterfront of London until the Crown sentences him to death for highway robbery only to pardon him on the coronation day of a new monarch.

What makes this work so durable is the bitter, cruel, and relentless truth it presents. 'Who's the bigger thief — the snipe who steals your purse or the stock manipulator who honestly loses your life's savings?" asks Macky.

Strangely, the work has been a popular one and has lived through the centuries in one form or another, retelling the sentiments of Gay. Bretch, the German, saw in the work a perfect framework for representing the Weimar Republic, which was tottering when he began his work. Hitler was in control when the work premiered simultaneously in some twenty German cities. The Nazis saw in it a bitter attack on the Third Reich and forced Bretch along with Kurt Weil, the musical composer, and Weil's wife, Lotte Lenya (the star of the original production), to flee to these shores. Attempts to sell the opera to New Yorkers fared badly; even the German film fizzled. The 1932 production with Lenya was ignored. The 1945 production with Alfred Drake as McHeath, Zero Mostel as Peachem, and Libby Holman as Jenny, named first "Twilight Alley" then "The Beggar's Opera," had a score by Duke Ellington, but was another box-office bomb. The English film version with [Laurence] Olivier in 1952 was excellent, but no one went to see it. Consequently, when the Theatre de Lys production was announced, no one was ready for the bang. True, Lotte Lenya would again play the role of the prostitute, Jenny, but there was little hope for a run beyond a few months. The show was an immediate "smash." There were no seats at the box office the next day by five o'clock, and still the smash had to close because the theatre had booked another work expecting the quick demise of "Threepenny" (the work was Calder Willingham's "End as a Man"). It was several months before "Threepenny" returned to the Theatre de Lys where it has remained ever since.

It is epic theatre, shattering any pretense at realism. The music would do justice to Alan Berg if he ever caught the musical comedy bug — atonal, harsh, biting — and yet, not without a lilt. The performances, originally, were nothing short of magnificent. Although, from time to time, I have been told the replacements were weakening the overall production.

If you are planning a trip to New York this year and haven't seen this unusual theatre piece, I recommend it highly.

It's a classic.

One On The Aisle
October 30, 1959

if you re wondering why one on the aisle is being written in lower case this week please remember it s most difficult for a cockroach jumping from key to key to make capital letters and things like that as a matter of fact the only way im able to type at all is to climb to the top of the machine and hurl myself down upon the key with vigor permit me to introduce myself my name is archy and i am deeply in love with a sinewy pussy cat named mehitabel perhaps some of you scottsdalians remember my creator don marquis who first brought my story to the public in his 1927 book about mehitabel and me marquis worked on the atlanta constitution for many years and at night id sneak into his office and type out my woes and observations on the mortal world which when you come down to it is not too dissimilar from the world of lovesick roaches and glamorous alley cats like mehitabel

when old don kicked off in 1937 i guess everyone felt a loss because his book and comic strip were doing real well and even mehitabel when she wasnt out meowing showed some interest which for mehitabel is quite a lot but i guess a lot of people loved old don real well because some 8 years ago miss carol channing and mr eddie bracken sang an opera called archy and mehitabel on a record and it was so good that some other people decided to make a broadway musical based on it called shinbone alley which didnt do too well i think it was because they let the mortals dress like humans instead of insects and animals and not even mehitabel would stand for that but I must admit miss kitt acted and sang like mehitabel and in the show i did my best to keep mehitabel out of trouble but for all her kittenish qualities mehitabel is still a woman of the alley which of course is our world but no matter what my heart belongs to her course i know a cat like mehitabel could never take a roach like me seriously i guess you might call it a cockroach comedy all this blabbering isnt gonna please tim kelly who was kind enough to let me fling myself all over his aging remington but i just want to point out that this weekend thursday friday and saturday october 29 30 and 31 the newly formed scottsdale chamber opera company is presenting mehitabel and me in an opera called of all things archy and mehitabel they are doing some other operas too slow dusk by a mr floyd and r s v p by a mr offenbac

mehitabel is quite excited and so am i and i think someone should pin a big medal on the chamber opera company for having such imagination in the selecting of the works to be presented the opera will be very peppy because mehitabel is peppy and always running here and there and getting into trouble like the time i had to get her out of the florence crittenton home but thats another story

tickets are just 150 in human money the curtain time is 8 30 and you can see and hear me and mehitabel at the scottsdale high school auditorium i sure hope you come even if mehitabel says it makes little difference to her which always reminds me of what old don marquis used to say a cat is a very special woman.

i better rest now for my performance cause im getting mighty tired ive just enough energy to crawl from m to the space bar and so to nap

your friend
archy
for mehitabel

One On The Aisle
January 2, 1960

AromaRama, which opened two weeks ago at the FourStar Theatre in Los Angeles, is Hollywood's latest attempt to build a bigger, if not better, cinema mousetrap. Some time back, that devil at the typewriter keys, Robert Ruark, complained about an article he saw in a women's wear shop, a false rump. Foam rubber. Mr. Ruark's objection is understandable. No man wants to purchase an avocado and end up with a pencil. Take this AromaRama thing. When they talked about the smelly thing, I thought the idea interesting, but — "Why trouble?" Now it seems to me that this rump fraud has a counterpart in AromaRama. No one wants to attend a movie and suffer the effects of a mustard gas attack. These gimmicks in films have gone too far! Several years ago I sat though a thing by Arch Obler entitled, "Bwana Devil," in which a savage threw a spear at me and a lion rushed at me. I was soaked two bits for some crummy 3-D glasses. I couldn't slouch in my seat, else the picture became fuzzy. 3-D was to save the waning film industry, and for about a year the public was bombarded with flying ping-pong balls. I am thankful that no one spit in any 3-D film. Well, the 3-D mumbo-jumbo didn't last long — people got tired of leaving the theater look-ing like Ben Turpin [a cross-eyed comedian in the silent era].

This summer I witnessed a terror film, "Horrors of the Black Museum," in — believe it or not — "Hypnovision." Some headshrinker came on before the picture began and hypnotized (Ha!) the audience into believing that they would be terrified at everything that followed in the film. He asked for complete silence, but the brat sitting beside me kept complaining that he couldn't find the prize at the bottom of his crackerjack box, so I never got to give the Mesmer his chance. Last summer I attended the premiere of something called "The Tingler." Theatre seats were wired, so that at desired moments patrons might receive a slight electrical charge. Some referred to the whole thing as a cheap thrill. When this smell business started, I wondered how the ad boys would avoid the obvi-ous pitfalls when it came to advertising copy. Good grief — they haven't! The releases read: "First they moved, then they talked — now they smell!"

In this first AromaRama film, "Behind the Great Wall," a score of smells attack the audience. You can smell a tiger hunt, a Hong Kong street, an opium den, and a garbage-strewn river. It's more fun to watch the audience than the film: nose and nostrils sniffing and quivering, it looks like a colony of Peter Rab-bits smelling a Caesar Salad. The comments all but drown out Chet Huntley's narrative. Let's take that opium den bit:

"Smells like burning potatoes."

"No, more like burning hair."

"I don't know which, but if they don't turn it off, I'm gonna throw up."

There's no escape. Mike Todd, Jr. opens "Scent of Mystery" in "Glorious Smell-O-Vision" (I'm not making this up) at the Ritz in L. A. this month. Vari-ous problems have arisen like the patron who inquired if she might get in for half price since she had a cold, or the man who wondered if his asthma would be affected.

Forewarning from the *World Telegram-Sun:* "You've got to breathe it to believe it — scented movies are here to stay."

God forbid, because the whole gimmick stinks.

One On The Aisle
January 8, 1960

Arguments about the merits of Tennessee Williams' works inevitably termi-nate themselves the way religious and political arguments end.

Regardless of personal sentiments, it cannot be denied that Thomas Lanier Williams will undoubtedly rank (if indeed he doesn't already) in the field with Eugene O'Neil. There is no dramatist writing today who can match his imagi-nation, output, or quality. To be sure, we have a score of capable playwrights turning out "entertaining pieces," and sadly we must note that almost 50 per-cent of our professional theatre activity is devoted to routine musicals. But we have only here dramatists of stature writing today: Williams, Arthur Miller, and

William Inge. The others that showed promise (Lillian Hellman, Arthur Laurents and [Paddy] Chayefsky) have yet to produce a "Glass Menagerie," "Death of a Salesman," or on a lower level, "The Dark at the Top of the Stairs." Inge, certainly, ranks a poor third to Williams and Miller. His current showing, "A Loss of Roses," a reworking of his first play, "Farther off from Heaven," is most unrewarding. Williams has managed to have an offering on or off Broadway ever since 1945. His language is poetic, his situations imaginative. Not being a social writer like Miller, he has greater freedom and from this freedom comes his strength. His novels and collections of short stories ("The Roman Spring of Mrs. Stone," "Hard Candy," "One Arm") are cruel jewels that cut while they dazzle.

Many would deny Williams his literary crown: "He's vulgar. He's dirty. He's shocking!" Yet, should we turn our backs on Life as a whole and accept only the part that pleases us? It is not the dramatist's role (as distinguished from the playwright's) to entertain. The dramatist searches for truth. He seeks to show Man to himself, to strip away the darkness that would destroy Man if Man did not destroy it with the light of knowledge and experience. The work of the playwright dies almost upon birth (does anyone have a burning desire to see "Lightin'," "Abie's Irish Rose," "Life With Father," "The Leader" — all fantastically successful in terms of a lengthy run?), but the work of the dramatist lives forever: Molière, Shakespeare, Marlowe, Racine, Strindberg, Ibsen, Chekhov, Shaw, O'Neil.

Since Man searches the greater part of his life for truth and the meaning of his existence, the dramatist's role is that of a religious zealot or prophet. With his drama, he illuminates the darkness Man fights against. To the dramatist, the theatre is, indeed, a temple. If a dramatist shocks, remember that he has found something in life that is shocking. To some, the fact that theatre is becoming increasingly social, that audiences are asking for less illumination of their hearts and souls and more razzle-dazzle, is shocking. Perhaps disputed plays are not decadent, but the society which prompts their writing is. A dramatist reports life as it is, not as we would have it. Hollywood does that admirably. There was a period in history when the Romans turned their backs on their dramatist and demanded bigger and better arena events. I doubt if they were happy with the ultimate results. Theatre in its purest sense is life enlarged — for better or worse. Let's not blame "shocking" dramatists for showing us what exists. Better to view the work and vow to eradicate the evil the dramatist shows.

He who sings frightens away his ills. — Cervantes

One On The Aisle
January 15, 1960

The mystery yarn, through thick and thin, has always been able to sustain itself. There are some who claim that the first murder story was Cain and Abel; that this Biblical segment started the whole thing. Some will claim that "Hamlet" is naught but a murder-mystery melodrama, and theorists are prone to insist that the first true detective yarn is Poe's "Murders in the Rue Morgue," while the first mystery put on the American stage is "The Black Crook." Of course, the mystery yarn has cousins: the spy story, the gangster epic, horror story, science fiction fantasy, and the psychological thriller.

The mystery writing business grosses something like $25,000,000 each year. TV uses the mystery as a staple. The films, which for three decades turned out several scores each year (The Thin Man, Charlie Chan, Sherlock Holmes, and The Whistler series), concentrates now on major pictures that seem, for the most part, to lack the very qualities of melodramatic seriousness their early counterparts had in abundance. "The Scapegoat," "North By Northwest," and that remake of "The Bat" (a fiasco) can in no way, compare to "And Then There Were None," "The 39 Steps," or "The Cat and the Canary."

The popularity of the mystery yarn can be the result of many things. Are we, like the murderer, getting away with something? Are we releasing pent-up emotions that, if not pacified by the empathy we feel while watching the play, might lead elsewhere? Are we exhibiting masochistic or sadistic tendencies? Psychologists say all these things come into play when we take delight in the murder mystery, and because we know virtue will triumph and evil will be destroyed, we feel "secure" in our enjoyment. This is probably true. Audiences took delicious delight in watching Baby Rhoda in "The Bad Seed" knock off this one and that one, but when they found out at the end she got away with it, they were genuinely shocked. All of a sudden they didn't like the play. No fun playing for keeps.

Let's look at children's works. Fairy tales provide a good method for the kiddies to get rid of their aggressive tendencies. Those two babes-in-the-wood, Hansel and Gretel, have no second thought about evening the score with that old crone in the gingerbread house. In fact, they cremate her; then to celebrate, they dance a charming jig-step. Bluebeard is jolly good fun, too. When finished with a spouse, he chops her up and distributes her around his chamber floor. It's an all-time bestseller. Kids love it. Hold on before you cart your offspring's "Mother Goose" to the disposal. When's the last time you repeated a "sick joke" or chuckled at a Charlie Addams [creator of The Addams Family]?

Horror films out-pull almost everything on a 2-1 ratio. And three of the all-time money makers of movie history are "Frankenstein," "Dracula," and "King Kong." As far as audience attendance is concerned, they rank in the top ten! Personally, I feel escapism in moderate doses is a good thing. Certainly this is true when we check the mystery offerings at Valley playhouse. No word yet from the Sombrero on a murder mystery, but the Phoenix Little Theatre has packed 'em in with "The Mousetrap." Mesa Little Theatre dug up "Laura" a short time ago, and now the Scottsdale Players are coming up with a new murder mystery, "Widow's Walk."

True, adult melodramas in the murder vein offer added attractions: pitting of wits against the unknown killer, logical deduction and conclusion, and the before-mentioned empathy. But when we come right down to it, aren't "The

Mousetrap," "Laura," and "Widow's Walk" nothing more than adult versions of "Hansel and Gretel" and "Bluebeard"?

It is always observable that silence propagates itself, and that the longer talk has been suspended the more difficult it is to find anything to say. — Samuel Johnson

One On The Aisle
May 1, 1959

The Scottsdale Players have a society. Its initials are S.P.M.S., - the Scottsdale Preservation of Melodrama Society. A lengthy moniker meaning that the damsel with the long golden curls, the villain with the foreclosure notice and Jack something-or-other, all-American wishy-washy, need not perish from behind the footlights.

There is something noble about such a society. One existing to preserve something that just ain't anymore. Time was when the ingredients of an American play consisted of an aged mother or grandmother, a menace and a wide-eyed voluptuary usually named Octavia, Iphigenia or Blossom. American audiences from 1825-1900 took such a work seriously and delighted in a season that might offer "The Cherry Pickers," "Blue Jeans," "Strapped to a Cannon, But Honor Saved," and "Bertha, the Sewing Girl." Their enthusiasm knew no bounds if an "Uncle Tom's Cabin" was thrown in. Early advertisements indicate that some "Uncle Tom's Cabins" offered two Uncle Toms and two Little Evas. (I've never been able to figure out whether they both appeared on the stage at the same time or at alternate performances.)

It's interesting to note that these epics, which we kid today, were accepted as standard drama fare in their day. American theatre didn't start to grow up until the mid-twenties, due largely to the efforts of groups like the Scottsdale Players. Performances of Charles Hoyt's works were noted on the Broadway stage as late as 1923 (Hoyt was the king of the cornball school of theatre. He died a millionaire after authoring some 200 play scripts.) The works of Harrigan and Hart didn't die off until 1910. (Their epics emphasized musical interludes and stage machinery. Quite often "a rollercoaster scene" was billed over the play's title or leading lady.) No one likes to admit we took such pap seriously, but there is no escape.

The work that pokes fun at the old style melodrama is actually a mellerdrama — "melodrama" being a perfectly acceptable drama term meaning a play that is filled with exciting scenes and acting, presenting a moral viewpoint in which virtue always triumphs and evil is destroyed. The audience at a melodrama is never confused as to what is good and what is bad (Granny is always good, so is her Mary Pickford vamp of a granddaughter. Jack Wheaties is good, too. But the man who asks Granny for the rent she's been hedging on since the last pension check period is bad.)

All mystery plays are true melodramas but as a dramatic form today, with the exception of these thrillers, the melodrama has suffered the same fate as the little shows of the thirties and forties (shows that were good, but not powerful or smash-hits); the fate being a slow death.

Getting back to the S.P.M.S. — they've been making quite a name for themselves; premiering their works at Jerome's Ghost Town Celebration each October and winning Community Service awards. Charlotte Francis, the author of the work about to be presented at the Stagebrush Theatre, is the group's general and she makes a good one. Her latest meller-drama is entitled "Drucilla's Curse." It's a post-Civil War saga dishing up such personalities as Fauntleroy Calhourn (a goodie) and Rastas A. Titus (Try his initials). The work will be presented Saturday and Sunday (May 2 and 3). There will be all kinds of songs and dances in the spirit of the old Showboat revues. Audiences can come to hiss and cheer.

Personally, I have always been looking for the work in which the villain, his good nature pushed to the breaking point after letting the old lady live in his apartment rent-free for nine years, kicks her and the rest of her worthless, whining brood into the gutter. I'm afraid I'll never see it for purists tell me it would no longer be a melodrama.

It'd be an American tragedy.

One On The Aisle
February 12, 1960

For my dough, you can take the Misses Cornell and Hayes and the rest of the sacrosanct actresses who must suffer no tinge of criticism regardless of how weak or inadequate their performances, and curse them to an everlasting route of farewell tours, a fate, I feel certain, awaits us; I'll stake my blue chips on a gal named Fay Bainter.

Miss Bainter is now appearing in the Imogene Coca vehicle, "The Girls in 509," at the Sombrero. Unhappily, my acquaintance with Fay Bainter has consisted of watching her in some half-dozen films, two or three TV works, and four stage plays, none of them worthy of her unique talent. The plays: "In the Next Half Hour," "Gayden," "O Mistress Mine," and "Lentil." In the first two, plays not without merit, Miss Bainter suffered only because the play of "less-than-tremendous-impact" seems to have no place on the American stage today. If "Hour" and "Gayden" had appeared in the thirties or even in the very early forties, their success would have been definite, but in an era of loud, booming, overpowering theatricals, the entrance of these works was quiet, and a quiet though good "little" play is a present-day theatrical taboo. "Mistress," a vehicle for the Lunts, was, of course, Coward by way of Rattigan, but a very profitable bit of chic hokum. "Lentil" is yet another side of the coin.

"Lentil" can lay claim to being the worst play ever written. Authored by Mrs. Ben Hecht, Rose Caylor, the work is an impossible bowl of metaphysical mush.

I saw it six times. Not wholly from choice, I just happened to be working in the playhouse it premiered in during one hot week in a Boston summer. What fascinated me about "Lentil" was Miss Bainter's performance in such a hopeless cause. Her portrayal in a role that would defeat a Hayes or Cornell in their best days was nothing short of brilliant. The most inspiring performance I have ever seen, as a matter of act; paradoxically enough — in the least inspiring play I have ever witnessed.

Her performances are always subtle masterpieces: patinas of virtuosity capping boundless theatrical strength. She can play most any type of role, but I feel her forte is the female menace of gentleness: the most in "The Silver Cord," perhaps.

Miss Bainter's career has been constant, solid, productive, honest. She never cheats her audience, in contrast to the hoopla prima donnas of the stage who arrive in Phoenix proclaiming they are here to bring theater to the hinterlands and then proceed to bore the pants off their audience.

Earlier clippings than this decade will show Miss Bainter in the company of Minnie Fiske, Daly, Belasco. She even did Topsy once [a character in "Uncle Tom's Cabin"]. If anything dogs Miss Bainter, it is her material. I would say that Miss Bainter is an older dramatic counterpart to musical comedy gamut, Nancy Walker, who always is singled out for accolades as everything around her is damned.

O! — that some dramatist will do for Miss Bainter what Tennessee Williams did for Laurette Taylor when he wrote "The Glass Menagerie." If ever Miss Bainter finds that playwright or dramatist or if ever that playwright or dramatist finds Miss Bainter, I want a ticket for opening night at any price!

Play Synopses

Widow's Walk, written in 1960

Note: The term "Widow's Walk" is native to New England. A widow's walk, in the architectural sense, is a small balcony atop a house that faces the open sea. In the days of the whaling vessels, most of the houses along the New England Coast had these balcony-like promenades. These "walks" enabled the women to see if their husbands' ships were coming into port. Unhappily, many ships never returned; but the women continued to walk the balconies in hopes that the ships were merely delayed. Literally, a widow was walking — hence the term "Widow's Walk."

Situated off the rugged, rock-bound coast of Main is Widow's Walk Island, a remote, forbidding spot reputed to be haunted by the ghost of a famed whaler of the 1840's, Captain Josiah Osgood (nicknamed "The Fisherman"), and the spirit of his strange young Polynesian bride.

For many years, this island refuge has been inhabited solely by the elderly and salty-tongued Mrs. Parkhurst, with only the sound of the gulls and the waves and the chatter of a hired girl for company. On an eerie, stormy night in February — almost at the opening of the curtain — the Phantom Fisherman traps the hired girl, Doris Ingersoll, and methodically strangles her. Then, for a different reason than the audience is led to suspect, he conceals the body and returns to stalk the wind-swept, wave-washed island.

Others come to Widow's Walk: Mrs. Maxwell, a bitter, stone-faced woman who conceals a frightening secret; Janet Hale, a vivacious young actress persuaded to take the hired girl's place by her boyfriend, Tom Peabody, a writer who wants a convincing excuse to visit the island — or so he *says*. Then there's a mysterious caller, Mr. Seyton (pronounced "Satan") who comes in answer to an odd "Room-and-Board" advertisement in a local paper, an ad that specifies that the "Gentleman must be interested in rock formations and geology" — an ad that Mrs. Parkhurst definitely did not place!

And, of course, there's the local law-enforcement official, Sheriff Perkins, and his amiable deputy, George Osgood, who are never far from the island's storm-lashed shore, pursuing lobster pirates or perhaps their own personal ambitions which eventually spell out intrigue and terror.

Then suddenly, the body of the missing hired girl is discovered beneath the giant grist-wheel which supplies the island's electricity. The action churns into high gear! Nautical superstitions, cunning smugglers, and doughty New Englanders clash head-on! The lights fail, eerie sounds whisper across the island, unseen hands cast boats adrift during a wild storm, "The Fisherman" prowls the house, triggering more baffling events and more spine-tingling deaths — all finally culminating in a nerve-shattering climax that is totally unforeseen and as electrifying as a bolt of lightning.

Teenage Night of Living Horror

It's WILD! It's WEIRD! The funniest movie spoof to hit the stage in years! If you dig classic horror flicks like *Night of the Living Dead*, *The Return of the Living Dead, Part II*, and *Cemetery High*, you'll die laughing (almost) over this SHRIEK AND SHUDDER FUNFEST.

Howie, Louise, Gary and Phoebe are in charge of "Ghoul Night," the annual senior class party. They locate an abandoned farmhouse by an old graveyard. Actually, the house was once occupied by the creepy, crawly Dr. Thanatos, who tried to re-animate the dead (gulp!). Vivian and

PIONEER DRAMA SERVICE, INC.
Denver, Colorado

Anne show up, determined to destroy the party. (*They* wanted a "Sock Hop.") Enter a grim farmer who warns the kids that it's dangerous to stay. We soon discover why — ghouls! While the decorations go up, the ghouls shuffle from the graveyard. Cosmic Cannibals! It's ghouls versus students! (Just goes to show what can happen without adult supervision.) Before seeing this show, audience and cast members should take a Scream Aptitude Test. Watch the spoof race to a spine-chilling and hilarious curtain. The characters are a blast. Production needs are minimal. Easy to rehearse and adapts to arena staging. Great opportunity for eerie makeup with the ghouls. The perfect show for Halloween — or any other time. If you're looking for a box-office smash, this could be your night!

(Running time: About ninety minutes.)

Happy Boots

Wealthy Mrs. Fitzhugh, after many years, has finally located her long lost grandson, Alexander, working in a New Jersey pizza parlor. The likeable but clumsy teenager is a cross between Jim Carrey and a young Jerry Lewis. To complete his meager education and give him a healthy environment, Mrs. Fitzhugh enrolls him in Arizona's Happy Boots School. It's an institute that resembles a page torn from the Old West and its motto is "Howdy, Pardner." Despite the fact Alexander doesn't like fresh air and is allergic to horses, he falls in love with the place. Mrs. Fitzhugh's niece and nephew, Brenda and Chester, are also enrolled. They can't stand the place and they can't stand Alexander. With the help of a shady private investigator, they concoct a hilarious scheme that will force Mrs. Fitzhugh to disinherit her grandson. Unaware of the scheme, Alexander does his best to become a true westerner in the spirit of John Wayne. The big excitement is the upcoming rodeo where the school's honor hinges on winning the saddle bronc competition. Unfortunately, Alexander tosses aside a banana peel and the best rider, Duke Pottinger, slips on it and breaks his leg. It's up to our tenderfoot to take his place! In a wildly funny scene he actually manages to bring home the trophy! Ride 'im, cowboy! Fun characters like the weird gang from the Pizza Parlor, cowgirls and cowboys. Alexander even finds himself a gal, the spirited Peggy.

This is an extremely simple-to-produce whoopie of a show filled with laughs, outrageous plot twists, excitement and plenty of good western melody. Among the hit tunes: "Happy Boots," "Sagebrush Lullaby," "They Went Thataway" and the big production number, "Rodeo."

Terror by Gaslight

Here's a play designed to scare the wits out of an audience. Hairs on the back of the neck will tingle. Macabre and eerie, it tells the story of the respected Dr. Cyrus Norton, a surgeon dedicated to creating an "anatomical museum." The setting is Philadelphia, early 19th Century. Norton, a curious combination of Dr. Jekyll and Sweeney Todd, teaches dissection, but because the law forbids any "subjects" except those from the public gallows, he is forced to deal with the villainous Gin Hester and Scrubbs, grave-robbers and body snatchers. Deliveries are made in a large wicker basket with the words "Philadelphia's Finest Meats" painted on the side. It isn't long before blackmailers, outraged citizens and the police are scratching at the door and the School of Anatomy must dispatch them in order that the dark work continues. A slit throat here, a pillow suffocation there, a brick on the head. Even Norton gets it when his luck runs out in an electrifying scene that will have theatergoers shrieking in terror. Just as it seems Norton's work will come to a sudden stop, his daughter and the wicked Gin Hester decide to carry on "business as usual." The vicious Scrubbs is the first cold delivery! The play offers an excellent selection of acting roles and enough humor to lighten the mood, but the emphasis is strictly on goosebumps and chills.

(Simple set.)

"The Butler Did It!"

Here's a delightful comedy that spoofs English mystery plays, but with a decidedly American flavor. Miss Maple [sic], a society dowager noted for her "imaginative" weekend parties, invites a group of detective writers to eerie Ravenswood Manor on Turkey Island, where they are to assume the personalities of their fictional characters. The hostess has arranged all sorts of amusing "incidents" — everything from the mystery voice on the radio to the menacing face at the window. Secrets abound in the creepy old mansion. Why does the social secretary carry a hatbox everywhere she goes? Who's the corpse in the wine cellar? And how about the astonishing female who arrives via helicopter during a howling storm? When an actual murder takes place, each of the "guests" realizes he or she is marked for death. The outraged hostess offers an immense reward to the "detective" who brings the killer to justice. What an assortment of zany sleuths: an inscrutable Oriental, a seedy gumshoe, a scholarly clergyman, a sophisticated New York couple, an intellectual type who idolizes Sherlock Holmes. When they're not busy tripping over the clues, they trip over each other. The laughs collide with thrills and the climax is a seat-grabber as the true killer turns out to be someone else.

(Can be played as farce or humorous satire. Ideal for all groups.)

Magazine Article

"The Town That Couldn't Wait"
written for *Arizona Highways*, February 1963

Scottsdale, according to its Chamber of Commerce, is "The West's Most Western Town." But it could handle another appellation with ease: "The Town That Couldn't Wait."

Naturally, the question arises, "Wait for What?"

The answer: "Its own theatre and opera companies."

City planners generally agree that after a community reaches such-and-such a population it might conceivably support a playhouse; rarely, if ever, do they speculate on the possibility of an opera company. After all, if the two largest cities in the state, Phoenix and Tucson, can't boast of such a combination, why should the comparatively small town of Scottsdale?

The error in thinking, however, is that Scottsdale, from its contemporary beginnings, was a town impatient to get started with its performing arts. If population charts and statistics proved that the then hamlet would have to wait for its theatre, well, those charts and statistics would have to be overlooked for the time being.

Boldly ignoring reality, a theatre that would continue to grow with a fast-mushrooming population was considered. Considered a necessity, that is.

Barely had Scottsdale incorporated in 1951, with a scant population of 2,032, when a small group of theatre-lovers met and decided on a course of action. As a result, *The Scottsdale Players* came into existence.

At first there wasn't much to distinguish The Players from the countless community theatre associations that spanned the country. Their aims were the same, their hopes for an eventual theatre of their own no different from the hopes of other like organizations. Even the plays selected in those first years showed no overwhelming imagination that would lift them from the ranks of the commonplace. But it was a beginning.

Despite a plethora of Doubting Thomases murmuring, "The town's not big enough. The town's not ready. The town should wait," The Players offered their first production, *Life with Father*, at the inevitable location for all budding community theatres: the local high school auditorium.

Whatever the uncertainties, the initial step had been taken. Within a few months, The Players moved quickly to consolidate their position. Typical of the type of people The Players had then and have managed to corral since was Attorney Robert E. Young who dug into his own pocket and obtained The Players' charter as a non-profit organization from the Arizona Corporation Commission.

During the next few years, The Players considered themselves nomads. For a while they offered their productions in Sound Stage #1 at Cudia City, a location for the filming of western sagas, and until a few years ago home of a television series based on the exploits of the Arizona Rangers, *26 Men*.

The owner of the movie site was and is a colorful character named S.P.B. Cudia. In those early years, he probably gave The Players as much heart as anyone. A long-time showman in both the United States and Europe, he came to Phoenix in 1939 and relocated on the then nearly deserted land not far from Scottsdale. He planned to make some 24 films there and actually completed *Phantom Pinto, Buzzie Rides the Range, Let Freedom Reign* and *Trail City* before World War II put a stop to his production plans.

When The Players were desperately low on cash, he offered one of his sound stages, with equipment, free of charge, and absolutely "no strings attached."

"Many of the great actors whom I have known," he told The Players, "started in small town theatres just as yours. Anything — yes *anything* — within my power that I can do to help foster the movement you can be assured I will gladly do. All my facilities are at your disposal. If my modest talent and experience can be of help to you in any way I will always be here to call on."

S.P.B. Cudia was, in showbiz jargon, "an angel."

Grammercy Ghost and *Three Men on a Horse* haunted and trod the boards at Cudia City, but when TV filming began to increase considerably at the sound stage, The Players found themselves entrenched right back where they had started — the high school auditorium.

This time The Players began to select works that would prove their mettle as an acting company. "Civic pride," and "Supporting with effort," met vis-à-vis with a work of considerable merit: Maxwell Anderson's *Joan of Lorraine*. This play demonstrated that The Players could take themselves quite seriously where dramatic art was concerned. But if *Joan of Lorraine* indicated a talent not fully explored by The Players it also marked a declining line on their aspiration chart. The Cassandra woe, "The town should have waited," re-vocalized, and the troupe, drawing on small audience potential and challenged by mounting expenses, almost decided to call it quits.

Surely, The Players have some benevolent fate with them, for when things seemed the darkest, an old carriage house on the Scottsdale Community Center grounds was given them with the provision that they fix it up according to their needs.

The "old carriage house" consisted of three walls and something loosely referred to as "the roof." Slowly, The Players set to work. On weekends and evenings a community effort poured a concrete floor, built a dressing room, costume room, storage space; put in a light board, installed a lighting system and contributed furniture, costumes and props. When remodeling was completed, at least for a spell, the "old carriage house" was rechristened the Stagebrush Theatre. The fact that a door in the rear of a set often opened straight onto the parking lot was passed off as a "novel approach," necessity being the mother of invention.

Play reviewers to this day find themselves at a loss to describe this "old carriage house," a designation that implies a certain amount of aristocratic neglect, if not charm. Terms like "atmospheric," "ramshackle," "funny," "homespun," "barnlike," have all been called into service. Quoting from one review, whose author had visited the Stagebrush for the first time: "The intimacy of the house also contributes a great deal to the fun. A tiny shack-like structure that holds less than 100, the Stagebrush offers last-row seats that are closer to the stage than orchestra seats in many theatres. The orchestra seat holders can prop their feet on the low stage." This last observation, describing a condition which delights members of the audience, is greeted by cast members with a fair amount of understandable chagrin.

Today, Stagebrush, while still "ramshackle," "tiny," "funny," and "homespun" can sit 150. The more-than-adequate stage is a far cry from those impossible early "carriage house" days, and settings are often astonishingly good considering the rather confining quarters. If there is something The Players can pride themselves on, it's surmounting the obstacles.

Rather than rushing ahead with a program of full-length works, The Players concentrated on "Workshop" meetings, sessions that continue even today. The "Workshop" is one of the branches of the Stagebrush Theatre that enables it to call itself a community theatre with honest conviction. Once a month a program is offered that usually includes a speaker, casting of a one-act play, presentation of a playlet and a discussion period that considers the production, pro and con. With its Workshop, Stagebrush gives an opportunity for potential directors to try their hand before moving on to a major work. The same opportunities for experimentation are given to latent actors, who might hesitate to "jump in" all at once and would prefer to build up some experience.

The Workshop gives ample chance for a performer, director or playwright *to fail*, a common occurrence in these sessions. This open permissiveness causes some members of other community theatres frequently to raise a dubious, if not outraged, eyebrow of incredulousness.

One of the strengths of Stagebrush Theatre lies in the fact it is not restricted in its scope. The Players' bill of fare falls into no pattern, no regimentation, no routine. Arizona boasts countless community theatres that present a "particular type of season." The Phoenix Little Theatre, for example, concentrates substantially on Broadway works of proven commercial value, while a group like the Arizona Repertory Theatre, also based in Phoenix, prefers works that, although they may have dubious value on the commercial market, rarely are in doubt as to literary worth. The Players draw no such lines, nor, for that matter, does their operatic counterpart, the Scottsdale Chamber Opera Company.

In any given season you are likely to see a monumental work such as Arthur Miller's *Death of a Salesman*, followed by "An Old-Fashioned Meller-drammer," complete with rinky-dink piano, dastardly villain and saccharine heroine. A light comedy, *The Reluctant Debutante*, is likely to find itself following Seán O'Casey's *Juno and the Paycock*. An original mystery-thriller shares the month with three one-act plays by Tennessee Williams.

The Players delight in *firsts*. In addition to the countless original works they continue to offer for Central Arizona, they were the first to offer *Salesman*, after other groups feared the undertaking. The *first* to present the work of O'Casey, Ionesco, Gressicker, and the Capek brothers, the *first* to take a gamble on something like Gordon Jenkins' never-performed musical, *Seven Dreams*.

The Players often stumble, but they never hesitate to place a bet in the gamble of theatre, even on a long shot.

Perhaps it is this refusal to be limited that enables The Players and the Scottsdale Chamber Opera to bustle with a creative activity that would have gladdened the heart of the late Robert Benchley, who took a very dim view of community theatres, indeed: "How come they're always doing the same play?"

Classics, comedies, tragedies, rarely performed plays, musicals, new works, children's plays, mysteries, melodramas and dramatic readings are all given bunk space at Stagebrush.

"That's what I like best about The Players--you never know what to expect. There's always something new, something different going on in that place."

This shunning of the mundane might account for the exceptionally high percentage of excellent critical notices Stagebrush has received. But if The Players pay little attention to the "cultural" aspects of their operation in relation to the community, usually being too occupied "doing" rather than "talking," they have a fine civic awareness that frequently, in their eyes, is more farsighted than the city fathers who recently built a municipal swimming pool so close to the popular playhouse that it had to relocate its entrances or ask its audiences to swim in.

In fact, over the years, The Players have waged something of a continual battle with the town's sundry administrators to insure their continuance; one staunch supporter of Stagebrush wrote to a local paper: "It is generally conceded by critics and theatre buffs that The Players consistently produce drama at least the equal of any theatre in the Valley with the possible exception of the Sombrero (Arizona's lone professional playhouse). And all this for one buck admission! These plays have been produced under terrific handicaps such as scorpions on stage, makeshift stage facilities, leaky roof with resultant wet costumes and props, $50 production budgets.

"In spite of this, a handful of dedicated people have been bringing good theatre to Scottsdale and spreading its fame. The land our theatre sits on belongs to the city. We could be thrown off tomorrow. During the time the property was owned by the Coordinating Council, we were the only member that ever contributed one dime to the upkeep of the area, and we were overjoyed when the city acquired the land. We felt that, at last, we might have a spot of our own on which to build a theatre. Twice we negotiated with city managers only to have them fired immediately afterward. In fact, we've begun to think that we are the kiss of death on managers."

Even to this day, The Players, unlike most community theatres, are merely "guests" on the Center grounds. But their desire for *Lebensraum* is one shared by the people of Scottsdale and there is considerable positive discussion and proposal for a land grant among the town's citizenry, who desire The Players to be fully secure and independent.

The Players delight in presenting western dramas, which emphasize that in Scottsdale's Shibboleth, "The West's Most Western Town," there is, at least, a brand of theatrical entertainment for substantiation.

Works like *The Calaboose Tree* and *Gentleman Jane*, segments of western lore by Hollywood writer Vic Panek, premiered at Stagebrush, and each year an original melodrama, usually the work of Scottsdale's Charlotte Francis, is performed in commemoration of the days when the West saw its "drammer" behind kerosene or candle footlights, usually in one of many local saloons.

For any number of years, The Players took their original "meller-drammers" to the ghost town of Jerome to help celebrate that legendary enclave's "Spook Night," an occasion when former residents returned to renew old acquaintants. The performances usually played on a continuous basis all day and night, a circumstance that delighted Jeromeans while putting The Players' stamina to the test.

The Players, in an era that finds critics seriously worried over the lack of theatres, professional or community, in which new playwrights can test their efforts, have cause for pride. Stagebrush Theatre has produced, since its beginning, more original plays *than all other community theatres in Arizona combined.*

They show their interest in this facet of theatre by paying the writers for their material, a circumstance that is by no means universal with community theatres.

There is a feeling, not without justification, that a new work by an Arizonian that possesses merit, stands a much better chance of being presented by The Players than a Broadway hit.

When they began, a run of two or three performances was standard. A few years ago this was extended to five and six. Now a play with a run of ten performances causes no surprise. If that play is an original, as is often the case, it's all one and the same to The Players; all part of the theatrical game they play.

The list of originals is lengthy and some plays like *Widow's Walk* and *The Burning Man*, which had their first performances in the "old carriage house" are now published and ready for production in other playhouses throughout the United States, England and Canada.

Yet, for all its contributions to Scottsdale along theatrical lines, The Players boast a thriving and pleasing social side. During the summer months, a barbecue outside the theatre often precedes a performance. Members of The Players engage in any number of extra-theatre activities: fund raising luncheons; swim parties, dances--just about anything that provides enjoyment. Anyone is welcomed to become part of the fun. The Players pride themselves in being a free and easy organization. While they aim to give their audiences the best show possible, they are likely to enjoy themselves too. More than once in any given season, they are likely to put on a play that appeals to them tremendously, even though they realize much of the audience might not share their enthusiasm. This viewpoint is much the same as one held by the old University Players, a troupe that spawned Henry Fonda, Norris Houghton, Joshua Logan, Mildred Natwick, Margaret Sullavan and Bretaigne Windust. The University Players had their "shack-like" structure on the sand dunes of Cape Cod and with ease and assurance followed the path "One for the audience and one for us."

The Scottsdale Players see this as a perfectly acceptable way to run Stagebrush.

The town's magazine-newspaper, *The Arizonian*, printed not too long ago this suggestion for anyone newly arrived in Scottsdale: "Suppose you were new in our community. Suppose you were looking for lively, interesting people to be with--people who do worthwhile things with enthusiasm, and have fun in the doing. Our recommendation: We wouldn't hesitate; we would urge you to become acquainted with The Scottsdale Players. 'There are no words to describe the intangibles--the warmth, the fellowship, fun and spirit that we derive from striving for a goal as a group,' they say of themselves--and hasten to invite the rest to come join them."

The Players have earned a reputation for quiet sincerity. The airs, pretenses, and nonsense are left to others. A leading director of the Arizona Repertory Theatre, Bob Aden, expressed it this way: "I think what I admire most about the Scottsdale Players is the absence of pretentiousness. They are truly a community theatre composed of amateurs in the original sense of the word. They are also very much aware of their limitations; work, and play hard at whatever they do, attempting to improve the quality of production, and rarely delude themselves with stuffy phrases about cultural contributions."

There is a strong tie-in between The Players and the Scottsdale Chamber Opera Theatre, an ensemble founded with the intent of supplying intimate, small-scaled operatic works in English to the town. The rise of Chamber Opera parallels The Players. Philosophically, socially and practically they offer a like past history, are aided by a similar supporting component (Stagebellies for The Players; Chamber Maters for Chamber Opera) and are unwilling to allow the vital creative forces in the town to go untapped.

Founder and producer of the Scottsdale Chamber Opera Theatre (SCOT) is a tireless individual, Joe Esile. When he first came to "The West's Most Western Town," he devoted considerable time to staging one-act operas at Stagebrush, but his desire to expand his activities and to devote an entire season solely to operatic works led to the founding of what is Arizona's sole continually producing opera company. Like the early days of The Players, SCOT began, and still is functioning, from the auditorium of the local high school. But SCOT, too, has every intention of reaching out and building a new theatre, one flexible enough to encompass the wide, wide range of musicana from full-scaled opera to ballet.

Now in its fourth season, SCOT, too, overlooked the woeful comments of the doubters, who unequivocally announced that Scottsdale would never take to opera, whether it be sung in English or Italian, and that the Company had as much chance at success as a "barefoot dude in a cactus patch."

though many individuals felt they personally could wait for a more opportune time, the town apparently couldn't, and Chamber Opera opened in October, 1959, seven years after the founding of The Players.

SCOT's opening night is one not easily dismissed; in fact, members of the company express a certain fondness for what befell them when the curtain rose. A furious thunderstorm broke and the singers found themselves not only struggling against a deafening deluge, but before the evening was ended, the storm succeeded in blowing out the lights.

The three operas that comprised the initial bill are often revived by SCOT, perhaps, as some imagine, "for sentimental reasons." Offenbach was represented by *R.S.V.P.*, Floyd by *Slow Dusk*, Kleinsing by *archy and mehitabel*.

SCOT took to the town's theatre way with alacrity, shunning the overblown, the ostentatious and the false. Today, the company works hard to perfect, has managed to recruit some of the best singing voices in the state, and is perfectly delighted to throw open its doors to the unconventional work, freely expressing a fondness for new untried operas.

"Quite a wonderful thing happened in Scottsdale," noted the *Arizonian* after the opening, " ... Chamber Opera was born in our valley... here are quality, maturity and entertainment of a cultural sort... some of the valley's most talented artists are involved in the Chamber Opera, whose talents, ambitions and determination are fortunately with the best ..."

To match The Players list of playwrights, SCOT came forth with noteworthy composers: Bernstein, Wolf-Ferrari, Menotti.

Producer Esile found himself in a quandary after his second season. "Chamber Opera," in the words of SCOT's past president Rob R. McCampbell, "is a medium more versatile than straight dramatic theatricals, for it can encompass comedy, drama, the presentation of new ideas, the promulgation of old ones, and adds the charm of music and technical skill--all presented in the intimate drawing room atmosphere for which the medium was originally designed long before Mozart's time."

This idea intrigued a dedicated but small following. The ledgers began to point out a mounting deficit. Rather than cancel out the original idea, but not willing to go broke, SCOT compromised by deciding to produce musical comedies as well, a form of entertainment that was strictly in the domain of neighboring Phoenix. A western motif work, Lerner and Loewe's *Paint Your Wagon* was presented. It proved a natural for "The West's Most Western Town." Strangely enough, this work which belongs in Arizona as much as any other western state had never been performed locally. The reception was jubilant and found critics urging a longer run. By the time SCOT's next musical (also a western), Harold Rome's *Destry Rides Again,* rode in as part of the town's annual rodeo, Parada del Sol, it was clearly evident that SCOT had assembled one of the finest theatre orchestras in Arizona, along with expert choreographers and designers.

Wrote one reviewer, after praising SCOT's ability to muster considerable style for their musical, "... After all, who could ask more from a group whose prime concern is opera and who must hit the tambourine circuit only to stock its chamber's dwindling treasury?"

SCOT's programming continues along divided lines, still offering its Chamber Opera, still entitled to recognition as Arizona's lone operatic company which offers a regular season.

In Esile's vision, SCOT will eventually be many things: a place to train promising singers, a trial spot for new operas in English; an Arizona showplace for the world of musical theatre.

If the idea causes some to wonder, it might be well to remember that in the space of a few years, SCOT has amassed a substantial corps of talented performers and its audience is growing with each production.

What amazes many veteran theatergoers regarding The Players and SCOT is the fact that neither group, from their beginnings, would conform to the pattern set by the countless theatrical groups in neighboring Phoenix. The feeling was, in years past, that Scottsdale would depend upon the State's capital city for its theatre and what little opera it offered, which was negligible. But the creative and artistic forces within the town were completely unwilling to play a second fiddle.

While both openly embrace the imaginative and the unsure, they are nevertheless solid in their business dealings; both are completely self-supporting, both have proven their capabilities and their worth. The attention they are receiving for a town of slightly over 30,000 in population is considered in many quarters nothing short of remarkable. For funds, physical equipment resourcefulness, originality and experience, the expedients have served them admirably.

But the most gratifying aspect to both SCOT and The Players is that they, in true western fashion, stuck to their guns when the going got tough and proved their point. Scottsdale had talent in abundance; it couldn't wait for the "appropriate time" to put it to use.

If you ask anyone interested in Scottsdale what the town would be like without SCOT or The Players, the answer, most likely, would be--"Unthinkable."

Their new theatres will be constructed within a very few years. They have to be because both these theatrical enterprises are determined they will be. When this occurs, the theatrical force of "The Town That Couldn't Wait" is bound to make itself felt on the national scene with significance not only for the town but, in the bargain, the state of Arizona as well.

"Creativity," Molnar once remarked, "can never wait. It is the most impatient of artistic virtues."

Scottsdale couldn't agree more.

Unproduced Screenplay Treatment

"She Couldn't Say No"
Written for Mae West in 1979

The fascinating and true story of
PURITY BABCOCK!

The magical lady who was responsible for winning
the American Revolution!

(Only the facts have been changed to make it more interesting.)

Principals

Purity Babcock	Pewtree
Irving	Governor Gage
Reverend Thinlip	General Washington
Ben Franklin	Medicine Man
Miles	Betsy Ross
Marie Antoinette	Colonel Von Sitz
Tularosa	Admiral DeGrasse
Louis XVI	

The action of "She Couldn't Say No" takes place in Paris, France, and the American Colonies, 1781.

PARIS, 1781.

We open on the exterior of a theatre, at night. The playbill reads:

AMERICA'S OWN
MME. PURITY BABCOCK
MELODY & MAGIC

Inside, the house is overflowing with an enthusiastic audience, mostly male, mainly aristocrats. On stage PURITY BABCOCK, an eyeful of a woman with a captivating manner, throaty voice and undeniable sexual appeal, is performing her act, a witty mixture of legerdemain and song. As one of her aides, a handsome young man, hands her two rabbits, she breaks into song:

> *These rabbits well could multiply*
> *A hundred times each year*
> *To keep their population down*
> *I'll make them disappear*

With a flourish of her graceful hands, the rabbits vanish from view.

> *You ask me how I do it, I reply*
> *The hand is quicker than the eye*

The audience roars its approval. With grace and ease, Purity materializes pigeons out of the air. Musical background becomes exotic and Purity deftly charms an oil snake. The audience is all eyes … and admiration.

Purity next places a man in an oblong box and proceeds to saw him in half. The performance is a musical and magical *tour de force*. At the finish of her act, at the wave of her hand, all her male assistants disappear. Now the audience really goes wild. Titled gentlemen rush to the footlights and shower her with flowers.

"We love you, Purity!"

In acknowledgement Purity replies in song:

> **Twenty Million Frenchmen Can't Be Wrong**
>
> *Italians are great*
> *But frenchmen are greater*
> *They kiss your hand now*
> *But they do better later*
> *They only live for women, wine and song*
> *Twenty million frenchmen can't be wrong.*

This time the audience explodes in reaction. The curtain comes down to a thunderous ovation. There is no doubt that Purity has Paris where she wants it.

Backstage Purity accepts the usual congratulations from her co-workers, fends off the advances of a senile duke and sashays to the sanctuary of her dressing room.

Her dresser, hairburner and confidant is a Gay Head Indian from Martha's Vineyard Island named IRVING. Purity long ago decided it would be un-*chic* to call him by his tribal moniker, "Running Water." Anyway, if we didn't know he was a Gay Head we wouldn't have to ask. He's the wildest Injun since Pontiac made camp. There's a knock at the door and Irving answers it, returning with a calling card: "Benjamin Franklin."

"Tell him to go fly a kite," quips Purity and suddenly recalls that it was his review some years back in *Poor Richard's Almanac* that gave her her first real break. Irving ushers in BEN.

The statesman is true to his reputation, a Renaissance man who can do about anything. [He is] gusty, hard-headed and practical. [He's also] a do-gooder who can't always behave. Being close to Purity is galvanizing the currents of his 76-year-old blood. He confesses that he has always admired her and is proud she's a compatriot. He flatters her skill as a performer, her beauty as a woman. Purity is enchanted and demurely hints he's too kind, that her talent is limited. She doesn't mention the beauty part. Ben replies by quoting from the *Almanac,* "Great Modesty often hides Great Merit."

Purity senses there's more to that quote than meets her delicate ears. [With] mutual respect established, Ben comes to the point. The American colonies, now ten years into the revolution, desperately need money. The French have been more than generous, but lately MARIE ANTOINETTE has been indulging herself outrageously, the result being that no more money has been forthcoming. Ben's powers of persuasion are waning. Perhaps Purity could influence the French court. After all, every man of importance admires her — even the king. Purity is flattered by Ben's argument and is only too happy to oblige — even if the Puritan League had her banned in Boston two years earlier for dramatizing The Ten Commandments.

"Illustrated slide lecture. I played all the parts."

All went well until Purity reached that one about adultery. She made it look so appealing that scores of Pilgrims made too much progress. As a result, Purity was forced to earn her living on the Continent where attitudes were far more liberal. She's more than sympathetic to the Colonial cause, however.

"I have always believed in life, liberty and the pursuit of happiness."

Ben, impressed, quickly jots these words down in his notebook. He asks if he might use the quote.

"Be my guest," replies Purity, delighted that someone is taking advantage of her mind. The novelty appeals to her feminist pride.

The next evening we're attending one of Marie Antoinette's galas, all glitter, bounce and cleavage. Marie is surrounded by her flatterers, army officers, fops — and her husband, LOUIS XVI. She scarcely pays any attention to the majordomo's announcing of various ambassadors: "His Excellency, the ambassador of Spain," "His Excellency, the ambassador of Prussia," et al. Finally [he announces]: "His Excellency — the ambassador of the United States of America — and Mme. Purity Babcock."

The mention of Purity throws Versailles into a tailspin and Marie finds herself deserted as every man in the ballroom moves to Purity. Marie, of course, is boiling. So are the other women. If they could just get rid of Purity...

Ben tries to present his case, but gets nowhere. Purity has no such problems. She's getting on famously with Louis. They exchange surface pleasantries and Purity asks who does his hair. Louis is fascinated by her worldliness, ability at conversation — and her body.

On the far side of the ballroom, Marie is doing a fast sizzle. Louis doesn't notice. Staring at Purity's décolletage he realizes he's got a couple of things on his mind and his wife isn't one of them.

Purity inquires, "How much do one of these balls cost?"

"A million francs."

"Hmmmm. How many balls do you give a year?"

"Four or five."

"All we're asking for is a million francs."

"True."

"Will it hurt if you sacrifice one ball?"

Marie has no desire for a direct confrontation with the rage of Paris, so she asks Louis what precisely the entertainer wants. When she finds out the amount she readily agrees ... provided Purity leaves with it.

In an ante chamber, the amorous ADMIRAL DE GRASSE brings word to Purity. He's entranced. Purity's not disinterested. He has a certain Latin appeal that registers. Besides, Purity has always enjoyed foreign affairs.

The spirit of patriotism burning brightly in her ample bosom, we next encounter Purity and Ben in a carriage, dockside. Purity is now an agent for the revolution. The money, in gold, will have to be smuggled into New York. The ruse is to piecemeal it in Purity's magic trunks, about thirty in all. Ben gives her last-minute instructions. In New York, she'll reopen a notorious Tory ale house, "King's Inn," a perfect listening post since it'll be frequented by loyalists, Hessians, British sailors and soldiers. The money will have to be sent on to GENERAL WASHINGTON, wherever he's to be found. Purity is to wait for a contact, someone who'll identify himself by quoting from Poor Richard's Almanac. Purity has memorized the reply.

Ben thanks her for all she's doing. Purity, as a woman who believes in freedom, wishes she could do more.

Assisted by Irving, she exits onto the dock where the thirty trunks are being carried up the gangplank.

Purity Babcock is about to join the revolution.

Bon Voyage!

NEW YORK HARBOR, MONTHS LATER.

The ship docks and to Purity's and Irving's horror, Tory custom inspectors are opening every trunk that comes off the ship. The overseer is PEWTREE, a Tory police inspector, a sour, sadistic brute, about as appealing as a weasel in a paper sack. Purity has met her match. She tries to kid him, implore him, flirt with him. Nothing works.

GOVERNOR GENERAL GAGE appears on the scene and stops his carriage. He recognizes Purity from London.

"But why won't you open the trunks?" Gage asks.

"They contain my magic secrets. I don't want to give them away."

Purity's gaze wanders to a public gallows and she swallows hard.

Pewtree flings open the first trunk and a score of rabbits scurry out, running helter-skelter, turning the unloading area into a scene of pandemonium as sailors and Irving try to collect the animals.

Pewtree continues on, undaunted. The second trunk is opened and a flock of pigeons explodes in his face. Purity appeals to Gage. Her "act" will be ruined.

Pewtree starts to unlock the third.

Purity cautions, "I wouldn't open that trunk if I were you."

He ignores this and heaves up the lid. A snake S-shapes and nips him.

Gage quickly accepts Purity's objection as valid. To Pewtree: "Now are you convinced? I have seen Mme. Babcock's act. She's an artist. Pass the trunks through."

When Purity tells Gage that she's come to New York to open an inn for the loyalists, Gage is delighted and in way of offering amends for the customs difficulty, he offers to escort her personally to her destination.

Pewtree opens his wound with a knife and spits out any suspected snake poison. He reacts quickly to Gage's order. After all, Purity has been rude to him, the ship was out of a French harbor and the law is specific on the question of customs. Gage orders him silent, guides Purity to his carriage.

Pewtree isn't satisfied at all with this new arrival and orders one of his bully boys to keep an eye on her.

When Gage, Purity and Irving arrive at the inn, they're greeted by a delegation of Colonial Dames and the REVEREND THINLIP. They're shocked to hear the tavern is reopening. In the past it was a place of wickedness, rum-drinking — and wenching. They appeal to Purity, for the sake of purity, to keep her place shut.

Purity counters with a song, explaining her lifestyle:

It's A Pity, It's A Sin

Now drinking is sinful, the good book informs us
Although it's delicious and soothes as it warms us
We feel much too good sipping whiskey and gin
It's a pity, it's a sin
It's a pity, what a pity

It's a pity, it's a sin

Wild parties are wrong, it's illegal to revel
And passion and love are both tools of the devil
What pleasure to fondle the form feminine
It's a pity, it's a sin
It's a pity, what a pity
It's a pity, it's a sin

The number goes on, cataloguing the sundry pleasures of life which Colonial society considers immoral, carnal or decadent. Before long, caught up in the bounce of Purity's *joie d' vivre*, the male listeners chime in at the refrain:

It's a pity, what a pity
It's a pity, it's a sin

The Dames are outraged and Thinlip unnerved. Working their state to her political advantage, Purity announces that she intends to give "performances," music and magic, sort of a "Theatre of the Occult," in the upstairs long room.

The ladies all but faint. One does.

"Witchcraft!" snarls Thinlip.

Since a plea to "clean-living" has got them nowhere, Thinlip appeals to Purity's sense of duty as an American to keep the place shut. Purity announces in a strong voice that she's a loyal subject of George III. Gage orders Thinlip arrested. Purity intercedes for him and the Reverend is off the hook. In a huff, Thinlip and the Dames exit.

Gage wants to stay and "talk." Purity has so much to do, is so tired. Gage, gentleman that he is, understands and kisses her hand. Purity finds him attractive — maybe even useful.

The Grand Opening of Purity Babcock's "King's Inn" is a smash. Outside, scores of men are waiting to get in. The disapproving looks of Thinlip and the Dames on the opposite sidewalk aren't very effective.

Inside, Purity is giving the barmaids and serving girls instructions on how to handle customers. "Treat 'em nice, but not too nice. The only thing I'm selling in here is rum and cider."

She tells Irving to keep his big ears open and his big hands off. The doors swing wide and the customers pour in.

To entertain, Purity sings:

A Minute Man Every Hour

I'm a wench who loves her lovin'
And i'm hotter than an oven
All i need to wield my strange seductive power
Is a fire that is rosy

A boudoir that is cozy
And a minute man every hour

There are times when i can glory
In the arms of some young tory
Who'll remind me of when knighthood
Was in flower

But a man with musket loaded
And the power to explode it
Is a minute man any hour

Watching husbands who philander
Here's a fact i've deduced
If the gander can meander
Then the goose can be seduced

I am partial to that gray light
Just between the dusk and daylight
At the moment when the twilight starts to lower
I adjust my time-clock's timing
Periodic'ly it's chiming
Announcing the arrival at my tower
Of a minute man every hour

Etc.

The opening of "King's Inn" is nothing less than a sensation. Ben would be proud of his, uh, "protégée."

In police headquarters, in a chilling sinkhole, where heaven is unkind to any rebel unfortunate enough to fall into Pewtree's hands, he hears his agents' report. He's discovered that Purity was quite a sensation in rebel-leaning France. Now she apparently has Gage under her spell. It would be quite a coup if he could show up Gage, whom he hates anyway. First, he must find out what Purity's game is.

The morning after the opening of King's Inn, Irving bustles into Purity's bedchamber. From outside comes the "clang-clang-clang" of a forge. Irving loathes New York. The men are louts and uncouth. The Dames are prigs.

"Why not go back to Europe where the life is elegant and *gay?*"

Purity really isn't listening to Irving. She's angry about the noise from the forge and decides she's not going to have that every morning. She marches out, gowned fetchingly in a flowing peignoir.

The forge and stable is right behind the inn and Purity approaches with determination. Her steps and temper begin to cool when she sees the stable crew. The smithy is MILES, a ruggedly good-looking chap with enough sweating muscles to shame Atlas. Purity forgets why she's at the stable as Miles carries on a friendly conversation. He introduces the men who work with him, each one a mirror image of Miles' physique. There's MARCUS, an enormous Negro; EBAN, barely twenty, who acts as stud groom; JESSE who can lift a carriage side with his back, etc. They're a good bunch of hardy youngsters, these young friends of Miles, full of spirit and idealism. Purity is beguiled. So is Irving. Purity pretends that she only wanted to introduce herself as a new neighbor, not to complain about the racket. It would be unwise, she says, to be an unpleasant neighbor.

"Who is wise?" asks Miles.

Purity is surprised and answers cautiously, "He that learns from every one."

Now it's Miles' turn to be surprised.

"Who is rich?" he continues.

"He that is content."

"Who is that?"

"Nobody," answers Purity, realizing she met her contact.

"So you read *Poor Richard's Almanac*?"

"I'm a charter subscriber."

In a backroom of the stable, the plotters discuss their plan of action. Miles and his men stand ready to move out with the gold the minute Washington's location is ascertained. Purity promises Miles she'll do her best at the inn

Hopefully she'll find out. They'll have to move fast because Miles suspects that Pewtree is on to them. He's right. One of Pewtree's agents is watching the stable.

Purity is fascinated by her contact man. The question facing her: Can business and pleasure mix?

That night, Purity entertains in the inn's long room — a display of magic that wins hearty approval. When her act is over, General Gage, at her invitation, visits her. He's enamored and Purity's able to worm [from him] the information she wants. Washington is in Philadelphia. She dismisses Gage with the understanding [that] he's to return for a "quiet supper" after the inn closes for the night. She sends Irving to fetch Miles.

The crowd at the inn is unusually raucous.

Purity does her best to keep them quiet, but trouble erupts. Miles enters and sees Purity fending off some over-eager admirers. He jumps in, fists slugging. The cry goes up — "Fight!" In no time the place is in an uproar. Miles' men join the melee, sailors pile in from the docks, Hessians go at Tories, Tories wrestle with Redcoats. The brouhaha is not only wild — it's destructive.

When it's over, Miles is unconscious. Purity has him carried upstairs where she can "minister to his wounds."

Not only is she a marvelous woman, she's a sympathetic nurse. Miles begins to appreciate this agent more than he thought possible. Purity doesn't object. Besides, it's a long time until morning...Unfortunately, Miles passes out.

The inn is a shambles. Gage apologizes. Purity says she understands and has a wonderful idea. Since the inn will be out of action for a month or so, why doesn't she take her "act" to the front? Obviously, neglected Hessians need relaxation. Purity knows the Hessian concentration is in the Philadelphia area. Gage is charmed by her patriotic fervor and leaves to take care of her travel papers, which will carry her through the lines.

Irving is not happy about the coming dangers. Besides, won't it look odd to have Miles and his men riding with her? Purity solves that. The men will be part of the act.

Meanwhile, Pewtree has received word that one Purity Babcock was seen at Versailles with Benjamin Franklin. He could arrest her now. Instead, he decides to follow along to see if she'll lead him to bigger game.

Papers in order, Miles and his men alongside, Purity leaves New York with the blessing and adulation of General Gage.

Unaware that Pewtree and his agents are tracking the carriage, Purity has slight trouble passing through the lines. Pewtree realizes that his own life is in danger as he gets closer to rebel-held territory, so he seeks out a tribe of Delawares and bribes them with rifles to attack the carriage and wipe out "the entertainers."

The small convoy is attacked by the Delawares. Miles and his men are quickly overpowered. The chief is a handsome young buck called TULAROSA. When he sees Purity in the carriage, his red hearts swells and he announces that she will be his wife. Killing her would be wasteful.

Purity doesn't understand any of his palaver. Irving does, and translates. Purity is appreciative of Tularosa's compliment, but she has other plans. When Irving gives this message to Tularosa, the Indians react unpleasantly and march their captives into the forest.

The capture of Purity and the others causes excitement in the Delaware village. The undercurrent of menace is wrong. Lives are at stake. The squaws are taken by Purity's finery and, in an attempt to win them over, she disperses her gowns and costumes, which they promptly get into. [The ensembles are complete with] powdered wigs and steel corsets, dainty boots and undergarments. Even some of the bucks join in. Irving is appalled at their lack of taste. What sort of camp are the Delawares running?

That night, the ominous beat of drums cutting the silence of darkness, Tularosa visits Purity. Irving again translates. Purity tells Tularosa it's impossible to be his wife because she's already married to Miles. She hopes the plan will work. Tularosa frowns and goes to consult his MEDICINE MAN, a grizzled old goat who has been supervising preparations for the coming torture of Miles and his men. He suggests that Tularosa engage in an act of courage with Miles — to the death. That way Purity would surely be a widow and the way clear for Tularosa.

Irving tells Purity that such an "act of courage" would mean the instant demise of Miles. She baits the Medicine Man, saying that she's a great Medicine Woman and will deal with him directly. At first, the medicine man refuses. It would be unmanly to "do magic" with a woman. Finally, she shames him into it. If her magic is stronger, they all go free?

Agreed.

Miles and his men are tied to stakes — to await the outcome of the contest.

The old Medicine Man has a hoary repertoire. His first bit is to walk on fire, a feat he does after considerable mumbo-jumbo. The Delawares are impressed. Purity counters the effect by eating fire. The Delawares back off. Seeing that he is losing his audience, the Medicine Man submits to a "test of pain" and sticks a dagger into his belly. Purity scoffs and checkmates by swallowing a sword.

"Now it's my turn," says Purity.

She decides to saw Irving in half. Irving isn't calm. It's been a long, long time since Purity has done the trick. Still, urged on by Purity, he goes along, screaming. The reactions of the Indians couldn't be better. They're struck dumb. The Medicine Man is furious; Tularosa is disappointed. The Medicine Man is a sore loser and says the magic of a woman proves nothing. This burns Purity and she tells the old man to get into the box to show he's unafraid. He has no intention of being cut in half, is shamed in front of his tribe, and Purity wins.

The tiny band arrives in rebel Philadelphia, tired and weary. They take lodgings only to find that Washington has left the city. There is nothing to do now but rest up and then plot a new course of action.

All Philadelphia is concerned about the whereabouts of the large British force under GENERAL CORNWALLIS. If General Washington could ever find that division *and defeat it,* the American cause would probably be won.

Rumor has it that Cornwallis is making his way to Brooklyn.

Admiral De Grasse, whose fleet is anchored in the harbor, is overjoyed to meet Mme. Purity Babcock once again and invites her to dine with him aboard his flagship. Purity would like nothing more except that she has nothing to wear. She explains the contretemps with the Delawares. To De Grasse, her lack of wardrobe presents no problems. His ship is well-stocked with bolts of cloth. He will send her all the material she wants.

Pewtree is afraid to enter Philadelphia because he's too well known as a Tory. He sends two of his men to shadow Purity.

Purity and Irving visit the shop of a dressmaker of some renown — MISTRESS BETSY ROSS. Purity will need several dresses and something "fast" for Admiral De Grasse. Betsy is not at her best. She's been commissioned by the Continental Congress to design a flag, yet everything she's come up with has been drab and uninspired. Irving agrees when he sees the creations. Purity offers some of the fine cloth De Grasse has sent along. On the spot, Purity whips up a design for a new flag. Carried away by her inspiration, she sings:

Red, White And Blue

Red is for passion
White is for purity
And blue is for love and lasting security
A star for each state

Full of pride, tried and true
Hurrah for the red, white and blue

The song continues, full of prophecy, as Purity tells of a future and great America. Mistress Ross is speechless — and ecstatic. It all sounds so right. Thanks to the cleverness of Purity, the seamstress not only has the design but the material as well.

She starts sewing.

Miles has discovered that Washington is south, opposite a large Hessian fortification. They'll leave with the first light.

On board De Grasse's flagship, Purity is treated to an amorous "supper for two." De Grasse adores her. Purity takes it in her stride. After all, they're both fighting for the same cause.

When it comes time for her to leave, hours later, De Grasse presents her with two homing pigeons. He'll think of them as love birds. If Purity ever needs him, or wants to send a "romantic notion," all she need to is release a pigeon and it'll fly to the flagship. Seems the fleet has been dragging its anchor in port for months. Purity is appreciative of the gesture: "It's so French."

Out from Philadelphia, back into British territory heads the troupe. They arrive at the Hessian camp and are welcomed by the lecherous COLONEL VON SITZ. The Hessians are looking forward to entertainment.

Miles crosses the line to meet Washington on the other side of a river. When Purity sends a message Washington and his men are to cross over, attack the camp and secure the gold, but Washington's advisors are leery. What proof do they have that Purity Babcock is actually an agent for Franklin?

the Hessians, that afternoon, are in a fine mood — eating, drinking, and carousing. Von Sitz and Purity converse — in his quarters. He thinks the Americans are a big joke. One Hessian could take on ten of them. Washington, waiting to see where Cornwallis will go, is a dunderhead. Purity continues to pour drinks. Besides, he adds, Cornwallis is moving on to Yorktown. This brings Purity up short.

"I thought Cornwallis was heading back to Brooklyn."

Von Sitz says this is nothing more than a ploy to confuse George. Some troops will move to Brooklyn and General Washington, thinking it's the main force, will follow. In Von Sitz's opinion, the war will soon be over.

A few passes at Purity, another drink and Von Sitz is out cold.

Purity is in a state of high excitement. The news must reach Washington as soon as possible. Nothing must go wrong with her plans for delivering the needed gold. Irving is to stand by to give the signal when Purity is sure the time is ripe.

The Hessians are getting soused and Purity entertains with "20 MILLION HESSIANS CAN'T BE WRONG."

The Hessians must have lead-lined bellies because their capacity for alcohol appears unlimited. Purity wants them to drink faster. Her own glass filled with cold tea, she proposes a long litany of toasts: "The Elector of Hesse," "The wife of the Elector," "The mother of the Elector of Hesse," "The sister of the Elector," "The brother of the Elector of Hesse," "The bastard son of the Elector."

After each toast, a Hessian is obliged to drain his cup.

On the opposite side of the encampment, Washington has assembled his troops on a riverbank ready to board boats.

At the Hessian camp the soldiers are in a stupor. Purity signals Irving on a near hill. He gets busy with the alert.

Washington sees a smoke signal and orders the advance, recreating his famous "Crossing the Delaware" maneuver.

The attack is a total victory. Washington is elated. He has captured all the Hessian equipment: guns, cannons, ammunition. With the gold he can now pay his ragged army. Purity tells him about Cornwallis. It would be the change he's waiting for, a blockade on land. If only the French Fleet were reached in time and ordered to sail into Chesapeake Bay and cut off Cornwallis.

Purity has the answer for that. Homing pigeons could fly right over enemy barricades. At first, Washington's advisors are cautious. [But] Purity is a woman to reckon with. The message is hastily written and attached to both pigeons. They wing upward into the sky. Purity will return to New York to carry on her work. Washington thanks her warmly, promises they'll meet again and orders preparations for the march to Yorktown.

On the outskirts of the Hessian camp, Pewtree's agents spy the pigeons and shoot one of them down. The message for the French Fleet to sail is signed, "P.B."

The caravan starts back toward New York, passing through British lines. Once over, Pewtree appears with a detachment of redcoats and an order for the arrest of Purity, Miles, Irving and the others. Things look heavy. Pewtree enjoys his moment of victory.

Under guard, the carriage slowly moves on to New York and a military trial.

In the Philadelphia harbor, Admiral De Grasse is delighted to see one of his "love doves" winging to him. The "romantic notion" means business and De Grasse quickly assembles his officers and gives the order to set sail.

In jail, Purity and the others are passing the weeks. Pewtree comes to Purity's cell and lets her know that her trial is the following day. His testimony will be most damaging — fatal, in fact. However, if Purity would be "nice to him," he might be able to arrange her escape. Purity isn't buying it, and denounces Pewtree for the louse he is.

He leaves the cell, vowing to see Purity hung.

"You mean hanged," she corrects him.

At Yorktown, the siege is underway. Cornwallis is blasted by Yankee cannon fire and French naval power.

Purity's trial for treason against the Crown is a scandal in New York. The British and the Tories want her head; the patriots in the city want her release. The cards are stacked against Purity. Nonetheless, she gives her defense everything she's got. Miles, Irving and the others are on trial with her. Purity knows she's fighting for their lives as well as her own. The magistrates are hard, cold men, and Purity's usual success with males is cancelled out by their ancient faces, uncompromising and severe. They'd undoubtedly burn her as a witch if they thought they could get away with it.

Purity sums up her defense in:

Comes The Revolution

We are treated just as subjects, not a nation
We are being taxed without representation
But there's a new day a'dawning
For you and for me
Comes the revolution
And here's what i see

Life will be bountiful
Laws will be just
And america will grow from sea to sea
Girls will be glamorous
Men will be amorous
And love will be free

Purity continues her song, painting a picture of a future America with the emphasis on the romantic. The courtroom is with her.

As for the judges, they decree death.

At Yorktown: Victory for the colonies.

Washington dispatches riders to spread the news. The war is over! A new political era has begun.

Gage visits Purity in her cell. He can never forgive her for being a traitor.

"I understand," she answers realistically.

"But as for being a woman..."

Purity understands his emotions here, too. Gage is heartbroken. He leaves Purity alone in her cold cell, waiting for the first light of day.

In the city square all is ready for the hanging of Purity Babcock and her cohorts.

Reverend Thinlip visits Purity in the jail and gives comfort. He'll stand on the scaffold with her. The procession of Purity, Thinlip and the guards marches down the cell corridor. Purity pauses long enough to speak with Miles and express her feelings.

"I would like to have seen more of you…"

Through the streets of Old New York weaves the procession. Purity is cheered and booed. At the foot of the scaffold the Dames she encountered when she opened the inn are contrite. They ask Purity to forgive them.

"That's all right, ladies. It's not always easy to recognize a good woman."

Miles is in torment, tries to break away, but it's no good. Irving is in tears and Gage is grim. Only Pewtree seems to be enjoying the spectacle.

"Wait!" yells Gage.

He comes to Purity and asks if she has a dying request. If it's within his power, he'll grant it.

Purity thinks and then replies, "Why, yes, I'd like to have my hair done."

Pewtree explodes. It seems a reasonable request to Gage. After all, Purity obviously wants to meet her maker looking her best.

So, while a stool is fetched and Irving sets to the business of doing Purity's hair, the execution is at a standstill.

"Don't rush it, Irving, I'm in no hurry."

Pewtree gets a message notifying him of Cornwallis' surrender. He rips it up, hoping to see Purity hanged before the news arrives.

Finally, Gage can stall no longer and Purity mounts the scaffold. At the top, she refuses the black hood.

"Don't want to muss my hair. I just had it done."

Purity says a few inspiring words on liberty and the rough rope is placed around her neck. Off screen comes the VOICE of a rider, bellowing out his news: "It's over! The war's over!"

Excitement, hoopla and Purity is freed to a chorus of congratulations.

Pewtree, defeated, remains sour. He has to run for his hide when Miles' men go after him.

Weeks later and we're on a parade field. The Continental Army has turned out in honor of Purity Babcock. She has helped the cause beyond estimation. Without her there would have been no victory. Now she's to be recognized officially. It's a grand moment. Miles, Irving, Thinlip, De Grasse, the Dames, Miles' men, et al, are dressed in their finest, and beaming.

The ceremony is impressive.

Finally, the moment arrives. Washington is to pin the medal on Purity. She stands in front of him, proud and expectant. Washington is all eyes. Purity never looked better. The trouble is that there doesn't seem to be anywhere to pin the medal. The gown Purity is wearing is cut low, low, low and the only thing hitting George in the pupils is Purity's large, enticing, overly ample breastworks.

A year or two later and things in New York have simmered down to simple Republican life. "King's Inn" is now "Liberty Inn" and the lower floor has been converted into a pastry shop. Purity is in charge of the pastries. We observe Purity hand a box of sweets to a customer and wish her good morning. We stay with the customer as she exits the shot into the street. She passes under the sign: "Liberty Inn."

We zoom in on the lettering below:

"GEORGE WASHINGTON SLEPT HERE"

FADE OUT

THE END

AVAILABLE AT MIDMAR.COM

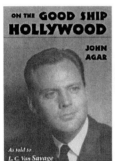
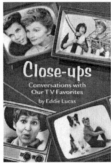

Printed in the United States
205108BV00005B/259-267/P